Journal of Latin American Theology: Christian Reflections from the Latino South

A publication of the Fraternidad Teológica Latinoamericana

2020
Vol. 15, No. 1

Fraternidad Teológica Latinoamericana
President: Eva Esther Morales
Director of Publications: Edesio Sánchez-Cetina
Journal of Latin American Theology: Christian Reflections from the Latino South
Editor: Lindy Scott
Managing Editor: Gretchen Abernathy
Graphic Design: DEditorial.com
Translations: Gretchen Abernathy
Editorial and advertising address:
Lindy Scott
1515 Riverside Avenue
St. Charles, IL 60174
Phone: 630-871-9750
Editorial and subscription e-mail: lscott@whitworth.edu
Website: www.ftl-al.com

Subscription rates: One year (two issues) $35 for individuals; $80 for institutions; $100 for institutions outside of the United States; single copy $20. For airmail add $5 per subscription per year. Bulk rate: $5 less per subscription per year for 5 or more copies sent to the same address. Address all subscription correspondence to Lindy Scott, 1515 Riverside Avenue, St. Charles, IL 60174 or email lscott@whitworth.edu.

Journal of Latin American Theology: Christian Reflections from the Latino South is published twice a year by the Fraternidad Teológica Latinoamericana (FTL), in care of Lindy Scott. All unsolicited editorial contributions must be accompanied by a letter of introduction and sent by email to lscott@whitworth. edu. Submissions in Spanish, Portuguese, and English are accepted.

This periodical is indexed in the ATLA Religion Database®, published by the American Theological Library Association, 300 S. Wacker Dr., Suite 2100, Chicago, IL 60606
Email: atla@atla.com
Website: www.atla.com

This periodical is also indexed in the *Christian Periodical Index.*

This issue is available as a stand-alone copy for purchase, ISBN 978-1-7252-7811-0

Printed and distributed by Wipf and Stock Publishers, 199 W. 8th Ave., Eugene, OR 97401. www.wipfandstock.com.

Contents

3

FRATERNIDAD
TEOLÓGICA
LATINOAMERICANA

The Fraternidad Teológica Latinoamericana (FTL; known in English as the Latin American Theological Fellowship) is a movement of followers of Jesus Christ. Since its beginning in 1970, it has promoted spaces for theological reflection and action contextualized within our wonderful, yet hurting, Latin America. The diversity of the Christian community and a commitment to the kingdom of God and its implementation in the life and mission of the Latin American church characterize our gatherings of fellowship and dialogue.

We yearn for a Latin American church that, transformed by the Word and the Spirit into an agent of the kingdom of God and God's justice, ministers in every area of society.

The FTL, as part of the church, provides opportunities for dialogue and biblical-theological reflection from Latin America.

Objectives

- To promote reflection on the gospel and on its significance for human beings and Latin American society. Toward this end, the FTL stimulates the development of an evangelical thinking that is attentive to the questions of life within a Latin American context. The FTL recognizes the normative character of the Bible as the written Word of God and seeks to listen, under the Holy Spirit's direction, to the biblical message in relation to the relativities of our concrete situations.

- To create a framework for dialogue among people who confess Jesus Christ as Lord and Savior and who are willing to reflect biblically in order to communicate the gospel within Latin American cultures.

- To contribute to the life and mission of the evangelical churches in Latin America, without attempting to speak for them or assuming the position of being their spokesperson in the Latin American continent.

www.ftl-al.com

Warm greetings during these difficult times of the coronavirus. May we follow the health guidelines of medical experts while praying for more just, equitable relationships at all levels in the meantime and after this pandemic calms down.

In our fall issue of 2019 (14.2) we began a series of articles that analyze the current state of Christianity in various nations. In that issue we looked at Mexico, Guatemala, Honduras, El Salvador, Nicaragua, Costa Rica, Puerto Rico, and Haiti.

In this issue we continue that series. Our first article is an overview by Fernando Bullón which sketches out recent religious changes throughout Latin America. Bullón sets the stage to help us understand the context of Protestantism in each Latin American and Caribbean nation. He analyzes in broad strokes the conservative and progressive expressions of both Catholicism and Protestantism in their historical development as well as their current levels of political engagement.

One sign of a group's maturity is when it is able to examine its history and current situation with honesty, peeling back for others to see its virtues and vices. When we accurately know our past, we can better face the future. Perfecto Jacinto Sánchez provides this kind

Lindy Scott, editor of the *Journal of Latin American Theology*, is Professor Emeritus at Whitworth University in Spokane, Washington. A long-term FTL member and former FTL treasurer, he recently coauthored the book *Challenged and Changed: Living and Learning in Central America* (Wipf and Stock, 2019).

5

of diagnostic regarding Catholicism and Protestantism in his beloved Dominican Republic. After addressing the history of these branches of Christianity, he presents some contemporary challenges for readers: the need for sincere dialogue between social sciences and the Christian faith, the recovery of a clearer vision of Jesus as the God who walks alongside those who suffer, opening up more spaces for women to serve as leaders within the household of faith, etc.

We have two articles regarding the nation of Panama. In the first, Marina Medina Moreno offers a straightforward overview of her country and Christianity therein. She celebrates the relative economic stability as well as the culture of diversity. While discussing several key areas in which the church has failed to promote "the values of the kingdom of God in all areas of life," she also notes the many ways churches and believers are tending to the real needs of the populace. She charges Panamanian churches to "let go of the frenzy for activity and learn to focus on the formation of disciples who follow Christ."

The second article about Panama addresses a pervasive and unacknowledged sin: glorifying the cultures of powerful countries at the expense of indigenous cultures. In "Indigenous Communities in Panama: Brief Reflections on Ancestral Memory and Creation," Jocabed Solano helps counteract this tendency. From the indigenous Gunadule people in Panama, Solano shares some ways that indigenous groups throughout Latin America tend to be closer to God's heart in their treatment of the land than many in the church today. She dreams about how the church could more deeply "participate in Jesus's narrative of reconciliation" through partnering with indigenous communities.

Throughout its five-century history, Protestantism has played both conservative and progressive roles in society. In recent history in Latin America, Protestantism has generally been perceived as pre-serving traditional values with an emphasis on individual morality. The biblical and social sciences scholar Rodrigo Riffo has documented for us how, in 2019, indigenous evangelicals in Ecuador broke with that pattern. Lenín Moreno is the country's popu-list, left-of-center president but was pressured by the International Monetary Fund to implement austerity measures which harmed the country's most vulner-able sectors. Thousands of indigenous Ecuadorians, including hundreds of indigenous evangelicals, took to the streets to protest these austerity measures, and in response the president reversed his economic decision. Riffo reflects on the observation that "Social protest is the new face of holistic mission."

Eva Morales, president of the Fraternidad Teológica Latinoamericana (FTL, Latin American Theological Fellowship), has worked for human rights throughout her native land of Bolivia. In "Bolivia: A Glance at the Current Context," she teams up with Drew Jennings-Grisham, who has dedicated his life to the recovery of the memory and voice of indigenous evangelicals in Latin America. Their article reviews the political

7

changes in Bolivia since Evo Morales became president in 2009 until the current moment of political instability and interim government. They also trace the role of Christianity and indigenous spiritualities in public and private life, concluding with the "desperate need for a theology of tenderness and hope in contexts of violence."

Marcus de Matos uses the Gospel imagery of Peter denying Jesus three times as a framework for how Christians have denied Jesus at three key historical moments in Brazil. The first denial was the violent conquest of Latin America in the name of Christ with the destruction and enslavement of indigenous communities and, when they were reduced in numbers, the vicious enslavement of Africans. The second denial occurred when Catholic and Protestant churches alike supported the 1964–1985 dictatorship. The third is currently taking place, in which middle-class evangelical Christians are providing intellectual support for right-wing political movements. These movements often claim to be guided by God, yet their actions contradict the values of God's kingdom. For Christians to be salt and light in Brazil, they will need to recognize and repent of these three denials.

Seminary professor and church pastor Flavio Florentín describes contemporary Christianity in his native land in "Paraguay: A Young Population with a Hopeful Road Ahead." His country faces political instability, corruption, and heightened disparity between the wealthy and the poor. Certain regions have been

8

positively influenced to a great degree by a peace-seeking church, the Mennonites. While less than 9 percent of the population is Protestant, Florentín concludes that "The Protestant evangelical church in Paraguay, though still fragile and emerging, makes a significant contribution to the spiritual, social, and economic well-being of the country."

Pastor Juan José Barreda, writing with Diana Medina González, tackles the current state of politics and Christianity in Argentina. Quality of life dissipated under the most recent president, and the current administration faces deep debt, a fractured society, and mistrust on the international scene. Regarding their involvement in political issues, followers of Jesus in Argentina have generally landed in two groupings: those concerned with sexual issues (ex., antiabortion) and those seeking social justice for the most vulnerable. Barreda pleas for "rich dialogue and actions of deep-hearted cooperation between sectors" and for Argentina's divided believers to be "humble enough to learn" from each other.

Finally, Christian psychologist and poet Luis Cruz-Villalobos shares some tankas from his suffering Chile. The tanka is a traditional Japanese poetry style that consists of five lines in roughly a 5-7-5-7-7 syllabic pattern. Penned just before the October uprisings in Chile, these verses proved both descriptive and prophetic regarding his country burning and "clamoring for full justice."

9

Our upcoming fall issue will explore the remaining countries of Latin America and include Christian reflections of responding to COVID-19 in the region.

Your brother in Christ,
Lindy

Religious Changes in Latin America and Concerns Regarding Protestantism

H. Fernando Bullón

This introductory article will describe the broad strokes of the religious reality of Latin America as a way of better understanding the context of each country in particular. We will start with basic demographic data and established religious expressions before focusing on Protestant involvement in social and ethical issues. Our historical sketch will be brief as we focus mainly on the current moment and its urgent challenges.

H. Fernando Bullón, originally from Peru, is the Regional Coordinator for Latin America of the International Network for Christian Higher Education (INCHE, formerly IAPCHE). He received his PhD at the Faculty of Economics and Social Studies of the University of Manchester, UK. He is a member of the FTL and an author of works that link mission, ethics, development, and Latin American studies.

11

Transformations in Demographic Composition

While Latin America is a region whose population identifies by and large as Catholic, religious affiliation has changed rapidly over the past five decades. From 1960 on, the Catholic sector has lost between 20–25 percent of its ranks, most of whom have become Protestant. This transfer has been greater or lesser depending on the country. In Central America, for example, nearly half of the population no longer identifies as Catholic.[1] According to one of the most widely recognized Pew Research studies (2014), Latin America is 69 percent Catholic and 19 percent Protestant; the remaining 12 percent is either unaffiliated with any religion or identifies most strongly with indigenous spiritualities or other faiths. The percentage of Protestants increases to 26 percent in Brazil and up to 40 percent in most of Central America. In the Protestant sector, nearly two-thirds (65 percent) identify as Pentecostal Christians, whether they belong to a Pentecostal denomination (47 percent) or identify as Pentecostals in independent churches (52 percent).[2]

Since 1960, the Catholic sector has lost between 20–25 percent of its ranks.

---

1. Roberto Blancarte, "Panorama socio-religioso de América Latina," *Milenio*, January 6, 2015, https://www.milenio.com/opinion/roberto-blancarte/columna-roberto-blancarte/panorama-socio-religioso-de-america-latina.
2. Pew Research, "Religion in Latin America: Widespread Change in a Historically Catholic Region," November 13, 2014, https://www.pewforum.org/2014/11/13/religion-in-latin-america/. PROLADES also provides information by country up to the year 2011 based on CID Gallup polls, noting the process of change: a decrease in the percentage of the Catholic sector and an increase in the Protestant sector. See PROLADES, "Latin American Population & Religious Affiliation by Region and Country, 2011," http://www.prolades.com/dbases/latam%20statistics/latam_population_and_religious_affiliation_2011_regions_countries-prolades.pdf.

Established, though Changing, Characteristics

In the attempt to provide a concise, general presentation of some of the most evident religious and ethical-social characteristics of the region, we can say that both Catholic and Protestant sectors demonstrate conservatism and progressivism.[3] The first typifies the behavior of the bulk of the laity as well as a significant percentage of the leadership; the second is a phenomenon among specific groups or elite sectors. In line with conservatism within Catholicism, it is not uncommon to find popular religiosity that seems to retain near medieval characteristics (especially, but not exclusively, in rural areas) marked by syncretism and blending with traditions of the original people groups as well as with those brought from the Iberian Peninsula. These modes of faith coexist side by side with those of progressivism: more modern, enlightened, socially-committed expressions that spring from post-Vatican II Catholicism and lean toward radicalism (primarily in academic circles, certain spheres of the Catholic hierarchy, and active organizations and social movements).

The fact that some Latin American nations are secular states according to their constitution does not diminish the widespread popular religiosity. The

---

3. Two other Pew Research studies, which complement "Religion in Latin America," attest to this description. See "Religion and Morality in Latin America," November 13, 2014, https://www.pewforum.org/interactives/latin-america-morality-by-religion/ (public opinion data regarding sexuality and abortion); and "Chapter 6: Views on the Economy and Poverty," November 13, 2014, https://www.pewforum.org/2014/11/13/chapter-6-views-on-the-economy-and-poverty/ (analysis of public opinion data regarding poverty and the market economy).

13

number of "Virgins" or "Christs" of one town or another illustrates this reality, such as the Virgin of Guadalupe in Mexico or the "Purple Christ" of Lima, Peru. On the other hand, and despite heavy criticism,[4] the Catholic Church is still considered an important voice in social matters, a spokesperson and mediator in tense moments between conflicting sectors of the population. Also noteworthy are the contributions of Catholic universities in the formation of professionals, in fields of research, and in publications of social nature.[5] Thus we see both conservatism and progressivism played out.

Though some Latin American nations are secular states, the Catholic Church is still considered an important voice in social matters.

Trying to achieve a somewhat homogenous characterization of Protestantism is more complicated given its atomization.[6] Since Pentecostals make up two-thirds or more of the Latin American Protestant

---

4. Critiques are raised due to the Catholic Church's conservatism and regarding its sexual ethics. Its conservatism is closely linked to sexuality and the "prolife" (antiabortion) and "profamily" (anti-LGBTQ) agenda, realms in which it has coincided and joined forces with conservative Protestant sectors. The church's conservatism can also be seen in cases of alignment with neoliberal, extreme capitalist economics. Regarding the church's sexual ethics, the critiques come from the explosion of sexual problems within the priesthood both in Latin America and around the world.
5. The leadership of Pope Francis seems to have breathed new life into the church in this regard, particularly his emphasis on social and ecological concerns.
6. Several attempts have been made at different categories of classification. In *Faces of Latin American Protestantism* (Grand Rapids, MI: W. B. Eerdmans, 1996), José Míguez Bonino identifies the most prominent church traditions and currents, which he calls "faces": liberal, evangelical, Pentecostal, and ethnic. In *El protestantismo en América Latina hoy: Ensayos del camino 1972–1974* (San José, CR: INDEF, 1975), Orlando Costas identifies three types of Protestantisms: transplanted, evangelical, and Pentecostal. The "transplant" variety coincides with what Míguez Bonino calls "ethnic." In any case, it is common to identify three main subsectors of Protestantism: the Protestantism of mainline denominations (in which the liberal and ethnic or transplant faces converge); the Protestantism of evangelical renewal, or simply "evangelical" churches; and the Protestantism of Pentecostal churches.

14

population, the sector called "evangelical" tends to be identified with Pentecostals. And given this "massification" of Protestantism, characteristics common to popular religiosity show up here as well, just as in Catholicism. At the beginning of the new century, Arturo Piedra described a series of phenomena arising from the postmodern ethos in Pentecostal congregations: the health-and-wealth gospel or "prosperity" theology; ostentation and hedonism; recreation-centered culture or worship services as entertainment, among others.[7] The Pentecostal subsector has continued to evolve, particularly due to the growth of a new kind of Pentecostalism: neo-Pentecostalism, which makes ever more notorious forays into the public realm, as will be discussed later in this article. Yet, despite its growth and even with its ventures into politics, Protestantism still occupies a subordinate position in comparison to the "official" Catholicism.

The sector called "evangelical" tends to be identified with Pentecostals.

Protestant Engagement in Ethical-Social Realms Before and After 1970: Contrasts

Since the 1970s, Protestantism has become more widespread in Latin America in terms of numbers of adherents, primarily because of the phenomenon of

7. Arturo Piedra, "El rostro posmoderno del protestantismo latinoamericano," in *¿Hacia dónde va el protestantismo? Herencia y prospectivas en América Latina*, eds. Arturo Piedra, Sidney Rooy, and H. Fernando Bullón (Buenos Aires: Kairós, 2003), 35–65.

Pentecostal growth. Along with this growth there has been a change in the ethical-social tradition of Protestantism. The Protestantism of mainline denominations active in Latin America prior to the 1970s was a force of intellectual and moral reform in the continent, despite its being a tiny minority.[8] In contrast, the Protestantism that appeared afterwards was marked by a millennialism of the marginalized and oppressed who acted as escapist refugees from the region's social and political realities. This massified Protestantism functioned with a corporate mindset and assimilated to the model of a hierarchical, traditionalist state as inherited from colonialism. As this version of Protestantism reached the middle class and certain sectors of the traditional, mainline churches, it started to show up in the political realm in the client-patron way of the corporatist, anti-democratic governments of the day.

Prior to the 1970s, Protestantism was a force of intellectual and moral reform in the continent.

Recognizing the growth and spread of Pentecostalism, David Stoll asked three decades ago if the Pentecostal and neo-Pentecostal alternatives could offer social reform and transformation at the national and continental levels. Doubts arose from the apocalyptical emphases and scant understanding within Pentecostalism of the structural implications that change on such magnitude

8. See the *Journal of Latin American Theology* 6, no. 2 (2011), which is a collection of articles about nineteenth-century Latin American Protestantism.

requires, as well as other elements at work in this "popular Latin American Protestantism."[9]

In the last two decades, Pentecostalism has burst with gusto into the realm of social issues[10] and even onto the public scene on political matters. Yet it has done so rife with contradictions. This incursion into politics has been covered widely within mass media as well as academic circles. The analysis is generally critical of the conservative postures adopted by Pentecostals. Typically, these are fundamentalist postures in terms of politics, economics, and social issues, aligned with the right in neoliberal economics and with a restricted understanding of human rights: their own understanding of "prolife" as against abortion, against gender diversity, and against a nontraditional definition of the family. Some accuse evangelicals as being dangerous for democracy[11] or even for national security.[12]

Mass media and the academy are generally critical of the conservative postures adopted by Pentecostals in politics.

Already in the 1990s, there was a range of perspectives regarding evangelical incursions into social issues

---

9. See David Stoll, *Is Latin America Turning Protestant?: The Politics of Evangelical Growth* (Berkeley: University of California Press, 1990), 363–93.
10. See Douglas Petersen, *Not by Might, Nor by Power: A Pentecostal Theology of Social Concern in Latin America* (Oxford: Regnum, 1996); Darío López, *Pentecostalismo y transformación social* (Buenos Aires: Kairós, 2000) and *El nuevo rostro del pentecostalismo latinoamericano* (Lima: CENIP, 2002).
11. Wes Parnell, "How a Growing Evangelical Christian Community in Latin America Could Threaten Democracy," *Religion Unplugged*, July 18, 2019, https://religionunplugged.com/news/2019/7/18/how-a-growing-evangelical-christian-community-in-latin-america-could-threaten-democracy.
12. Juan Carlos Pérez Salazar, "'Las iglesias evangélicas son un problema de seguridad nacional en América Latina': Santiago Gamboa, autor de 'Será larga la noche,'" *BBC Mundo*, November 5, 2019, https://www.bbc.com/mundo/noticias-america-latina-50251069.

17

and politics. Some suggested that evangelicals needed to start off more in the grass roots: local community engagement or community-level state institutions, instead of jumping straight into the national governing bodies.[13] Some, observing the contradictions already apparent in Protestant political involvement, warned about the lack of training and adequate preparation for Protestants entering politics.[14] Bastian pointed out how Protestantism was adopting popular religiosity's characteristics of being reactionary, supporting authoritarian regimes, and settling for the status quo.[15] Others remarked on something that we still need to pay attention to: conspiracy theories that reveal external manipulation with ulterior motives. That is, the notion that evangelicals in Latin America are being controlled by the US evangelical right and their militaristic campaigns, which allows for a resurgence of old conspiracy accusations against Protestants, that they were agents of North American imperialism. We must pay attention when some in the current US government, through various public gestures of religiosity, demonstrate their evangelical ties (Trump, Pence, Pompeo, and others) and meanwhile interfere in countries in our region in a Cold-War style clearly

13. Douglas Peterson, *Not by Might, Nor by Power: A Pentecostal Theology of Social Concern in Latin America* (Oxford: Regnum, 1996).
14. C. René Padilla, ed. *De la marginación al compromiso: Los evangélicos y la política en América Latina* (Buenos Aires: FTL, 1991), 5–19; Tomás Gutiérrez, ed., *Los evangélicos en Perú y América Latina: Ensayos sobre su historia* (Lima: CEHILA-AHP, 1997), 207–34.
15. Jean-Pierre Bastian, "El protestantismo en América Latina," in *Resistencia y esperanza: Historia del pueblo cristiano en América Latina y el Caribe*, ed. Enrique Dussel (San José, CR: DEI, 1995), 474–81.

aligned with antienvironmental, neoliberal economic policies.[16] And many other critiques have been raised regarding the processes of ideologizing, assimilation, and confusion on the part of Protestants becoming actors in the political realm in Latin America.[17]

In general, for Protestantism to recover its role as an active force of social transformation, it needs to develop an awareness of its own history. It should recognize its former culture of radical liberalism that mixed intellectualism with spirituality and was committed to the transformation of society in light of the values it espoused.

Some accuse evangelicals as being dangerous for democracy or even for national security.

Development and Religious Backdrop: Concerns

One way to understand the religious landscape of Latin America is to contrast the ethical-social impact of Catholicism and that of Protestantism. This level of comparison goes beyond parochial discrepancies regarding dogmatic religious matters (beliefs, liturgical styles, rituals in general) to include the economic and political development of the regions where these faith expressions are dominant. In very broad strokes,

16. Stoll, *Is Latin America Turning Protestant?*, 363–93.
17. See the chapters on Brazil and Chile in Padilla, ed. *De la marginación al compromiso*; and Heinrich Schäfer, *Protestantismo y crisis social en América Central* (San José, CR: DEI, 1992), 189–233.

19

we can perceive different paths to development in countries with a primarily Protestant background (for example, the United States or Nordic Europe) and those that are majority Catholic (Latin America).

The path to development in countries with a Protestant background has been very different from the path in Catholic-majority countries.

Sky-rocketing degrees of discontent and divisiveness in many Latin American countries have led to a situation of multitudinous crowds filling the streets in exasperated protest. Various experts and international organizations attribute this wave of massive protests to heightened dissatisfaction with the unequal distribution of the social outcomes of economic-production processes in these Catholic-majority countries. There are vast sectors of unemployed people or people with incomes too low to allow them to cover their basic needs. The critiques fall squarely at the feet of the neoliberal economic system, which concentrates and centralizes wealth among a very small, select group. The promises made by this system to redistribute the economic growth have not come to fruition.[18]

Connecting this economic analysis with our earlier religious overview, we must acknowledge that the system in place when mainline Protestantism was making its contributions to the region's development has become obsolete. The "modernist liberalism" of the

---

18. In *Capital in the Twenty-First Century* (Cambridge, MA: Harvard UP, 2014), the French economist Thomas Piketti details his long-term, worldwide research to lay bare the reality of the concentration of wealth through accumulation (primarily inherited). He advocates for tax policies that allow for better social redistribution.

first half of the twentieth century offers perspectives that are inadequate for facing the demands of populations clamoring for a more just redistribution of the products of economic growth.

Currently, and with very few exceptions, the countries with greater Protestant presence (with the hegemony of the USA at the center) are precisely the more "developed" countries; yet they are also the countries promoting and nursing the neoliberal economic system critiqued for its tendency to concentrate wealth and to demand growth and consumerism with disastrous consequences for the environment. Conservative and fundamentalist perspectives that mix religion with politics seem to harden more by the day, to the degree that, beginning with the economic and missionary hegemon that is the United States and spreading south, the "evangelical" sector that appears on the public scene is perceived as a conveyer belt of the neoliberal economic system. This situation is so entrenched that the Latin American evangelical sector becomes part of the supranational structure and network of this neoliberal advance. Furthermore, the evangelical sector involved in politics demonstrates clear opposition to progressive currents in social issues and human rights. Evangelicals in politics nearly always appear as negators of the contributions of socialist currents, even those assimilated by the most mature social democracies like in northern Europe.

The "evangelical" sector that appears on the public scene is perceived as a conveyer belt of the neoliberal economic system.

21

Urgent Challenges

In this sense, reviewing relationships within Protestantism itself—between churches located in Latin America and between Latin American churches and those located in the USA with whom they maintain denominational and ecclesial ties—is urgent. On a local level, churches must examine the interactions of their members in the public sphere, keeping in mind the concerns mentioned here. On the other hand, Latin American churches must exhort the leadership of their denominations or church networks, located primarily in the United States, to also keep these concerns in mind and prioritize the formation and preparation of their members. Both laity and leadership need preparation and training for public engagement aligned with the holistic content of Scriptures and with the historical experience of the church in terms of social justice.

National problems will not be overcome without cooperation and joint efforts among all sectors of citizens.

The responsibility does not fall only on the shoulders of local and foreign church leadership. Recognizing that we currently live in plural societies with global relationships, and keeping in mind the previously described context of social unrest and inequality, it is clear that national problems will not be overcome without cooperation and joint efforts among all sectors of citizens. Since Vatican II, the subject of Catholic-Protestant cooperation has been a viable topic of study and action, and the various religious sectors must pour their efforts into working together. This cooperation must not be relegated to particular moral agendas but should arise in a holistic perspective (spirituality, evangelization, social action) for the sake of regenerating the social and cultural fabric of our societies according to the values of the kingdom of God.

A related matter that is a serious issue for our region is the struggle for truly secular states. Latin America needs governments that guarantee authentic equality between different faiths and their adherents in terms of equal access to services and participation in the development and management of the state in all its manifestations.[19] Protestantism remains in a subordinate position to Catholicism in this regard, and other minority religions even more so. Protestants have increased to be a significant minority and, in some countries, are nearing proportions almost equal to the Catholic sector. Yet in many contexts what play out are the laboriously enmeshed historical relationships of interference by and privilege for Catholicism that impede a fuller development and contribution from other religious sectors to the region's development.

A serious issue for our region is the struggle for truly secular states.

There is no shortage of one thing in Latin America: opportunities for Christianity, both Catholic and Protestant, together with other nonreligious sectors, to

19. Currently, Catholicism is still officially the state religion of Costa Rica, and neither Argentina nor Panama have clearly defined their secular status in their constitutions.

23

contribute in a decisive way to improving life in Latin American societies, with greater equity and well-being for all.

Christianity in the Dominican Republic Today: History and Challenges

Perfecto Jacinto Sánchez

Introduction

This article paints a picture of Christianity in the Dominican Republic. After a general overview of the country and its history, we will trace the history of Christianity on the island from the arrival of Europeans. As we will see, the relationship between Europeans and the native Tainos was one of imposition,

Perfecto Jacinto Sánchez, coordinator for his country's chapter of the FTL, has degrees in social sciences and theology, with a focus on HIV/AIDS. A member of the Baptist church, he serves as a regional coordinator for the government's literacy plan in the Dominican Republic.

25

as the colonizers gave no credence to Taino religious beliefs but instead imposed Christianity as the official religion. We will then look at the development of Catholicism and the arrival of Protestantism on the island. The relationship between these two currents of Christianity was far from amicable, as each represented a different mother country that disputed not only geographical space but also religious expansion and control. We will conclude with several challenges currently facing Christianity in the Dominican Republic.

The State of the Nation

The Dominican Republic (DR) stretches for some 18,700 square miles over the eastern part of the island Hispaniola, which it shares with Haiti, and over the numerous islands, cays, and islets that surround the main island. The country is known for its beaches, tourist destinations, and golf clubs. It is home to tropical forests, savannah, and mountainous regions, including Pico Duarte, the highest mountain in the Caribbean. The capital city, Santo Domingo, maintains the Spanish colonial style as seen in the Gothic Primada de América Cathedral. In 2010, the DR was the second largest and most populated island in the

Caribbean, after Cuba, with an estimated population of 10.8 million for 2020.[1]

Inhabited by the Taino tribe since the seventh century AD, Christopher Columbus laid claim to the island in 1492, turning it into the first permanent European settlement in the Americas. Columbus's brother, Bartholomew Columbus, founded Santo Domingo—the current capital city—as the first Spanish capital in the so-called New World, in 1496. After three centuries of Spanish rule—with intermittent French incursions—, the country achieved independence in 1821 but within a year was taken over by Haiti. After twenty-two years of chaotic Haitian rule, Dominicans regained independence as a nation. However, the country floundered with pendulum swings between abysmally run governments to progress at the hand of repressive dictators; occupation by Spain and later the United States; revolution and the thirty-one-year despotism of Rafael Trujillo. The country limped along through Democratic revolts, US intervention, and puppet governments until relatively stable democracy in the 1990s and early twenty-first century. The current president, Danilo Medina, is finishing his second term and has enjoyed unprecedented approval ratings while instituting many reforms and stabilizing the economy,

> *Inhabited by the Taino tribe since the seventh century AD, Christopher Columbus laid claim to the island in 1492.*

1. Data summarized from Howard J. Wiarda and Nancie L. González, "Dominican Republic," *Encyclopaedia Britannica*, last updated December 6, 2019, https://www.britannica.com/place/Dominican-Republic; and World Population Review, "Dominican Republic Population 2020," updated February 17, 2020, https://worldpopulationreview.com/countries/dominican-republic-population/.

though corruption and disparities still abound. Despite favorable economic indicators—the World Bank identifies the DR as the "fastest-growing [Latin American and Caribbean] economy" at 7 percent annual growth in 2018—the benefits of the vast wealth and production of the country remain out of reach of the population in general.[2] The country is preparing for presidential elections in 2020.

December 5, 2020 will mark 528 years of the presence of European conquistadors on our island, which is over five centuries of history that have wounded our land. Some pro-Spanish Dominican historians present this historic event as an encounter between two cultures. They disqualify the advanced nature of the preexisting Taino society to assert that the Europeans brought development and progress. Others take a more critical stance toward the nation's history and focus on what European presence meant for the Taino population: the blatant violation of their rights and human dignity.

The State of the Church

Historical Review of Christianity in the DR

A thorough treatment of the presence of Christianity in the DR remains an outstanding task for churches in

2. The World Bank, "The World Bank in Dominican Republic: Overview," updated September 25, 2019, https://www.worldbank.org/en/country/dominicanrepublic/overview.

our country, both Catholic and Protestant. There are no robust studies that follow the historic development of any expression of Christianity on the island, nor are there any books that discuss Christianity within the country to any degree of detail. Despite the scarcity of specific documentation, we do know that the arrival of Spanish conquista- dors to the continent set off the historic process of Christianity throughout the Americas.

A thorough treatment of the presence of Christianity in the DR remains an outstanding task.

To speak of Christianity in the DR, we must remember the broader historical picture and its impact at the national level. Before the con- quistadors ever caught sight of our island, the settlement of resident Tainos called our land Quisqueya and had lived here for quite some time. They had their social and religious structures and customs and communicated with their gods. Our indigenous peoples were polytheistic, believing in dif- ferent deities that were manifested in natural cycles, like the god of rain, sun, fertility, and food. Cordero Michel explains that our Taino ancestors paid tribute to their gods through totem.[3] The arrival of Europeans to what became known as Hispaniola had a major impact on Taino beliefs, given that the worldview of the newcomers was entirely different from anything the natives had ever encountered. It would be diffi- cult to overstate the role played by Christianity at the

---

3. "The religion of the Taino society was symbolized materially through totem. Totemism consisted in the worship and magic reverence of ancestors, mysterious animals, and the plants that sustained groups related by blood, whether *gens*, clan, or tribe." See Emilio Cordero Michel, *Cátedras de historia social, económica y política dominicana (HIS-111)* (Santo Domingo: Archivo General de la Nación, 2015), 59.

29

time in Europe, especially considering the marriage of Ferdinand II of Aragon to Isabella I of Castile: the Catholic Monarchs. Their matrimony effectively wed the church and the state, leading to the Inquisition which the Catholic Monarchs established in 1478 to consolidate their power by persecuting and sentencing before a court of law all those who had been baptized and had abandoned Christianity.

The Spanish conquistadors imposed Christianity on the Tainos living in the land the conquerors had claimed. The Tainos were at a disadvantage in this cultural encounter. Christianity had been developing in Europe for centuries and was a major player between other dominant religions like Judaism and Islam. On December 5, 1492, Columbus arrived on the island Quisqueya on his first voyage with a vast crew, including several religious clerics. Their arrival marks the beginning of Christian presence in the DR. Some historians describe the unequal relationship between the cultures through the image of the Spanish arriving with the cross in one hand and the sword in the other.

African-Caribbean spirituality began with these first slaves who arrived on the island.

The exploitation, subjugation, and forced labor of the Tainos followed the arrival of the Europeans. As the sociologist and anthropologist Carlos Andújar Persinal states,

The colonization process brought social relationships of production based on exploitation of aboriginal manual labor and, as a

30

consequence of the extermination of this labor source, of Africans brought in mass as slaves to the continent beginning in 1520. However, slaves had arrived on the island on Christopher Columbus's second voyage in 1493, servants of Spanish officials, part of the entourage, as property and goods.[4]

Our African-Caribbean spirituality began with these first slaves who arrived on the island. Taino and African-Dominican spiritualities are the ancestral religious and cultural manifestations that have been with us since the early years of Spanish coloniza-tion. Yet the Taino and African traditions underwent violent changes as the Spanish obligated the subju-gated natives and Africans to convert to Catholicism. Conversion demonstrated having received the true Christian faith upheld by the king and queen of Spain, and the Catholic Church authorized the conquistadors to convert and baptize the conquered peoples.

The situation was so cruel that, between 1492 and 1517, and as a result of exploitation by the Spaniards, the original Taino population was reduced to a small per-centage of what it had been.[5] The treatment of the Tainos was so degrading that Friar Antonio de Montesinos led the friars of the order of Santo Domingo to protest

---

4. Carlos Andújar Persinal, *Identidad cultural y religiosidad popular* (Santo Domingo: Letra Gráfica, 2007), 159–60.
5. Russell Schimmer, "Hispaniola," Genocide Studies Program (Yale University), n.d., https://gsp.yale.edu/case-studies/colonial-genocides-project/hispaniola.

31

Perfecto Jacinto Sánchez

the European atrocities in 1511.[6] Montesinos's Advent sermon, in which he accused all present of mortal sin against the indigenous inhabitants, is the first recorded protest for indigenous rights in the history of colonization. After the Dominican friars protested, the situation of the indigenous tribe changed to a degree, yet the same cannot be said of the slaves brought from Africa. As the indigenous labor force died off, the Spanish colonizers—unconcerned with the well-being of the Tainos and caring only for cheap labor in order to generate greater wealth—subjected African slaves to horrendous abuse, exploitation, and overtaxing work. Whereas the Tainos had been used primarily to mine for gold, African manual labor was focused on planting and harvesting sugar cane.

A friar's 1511 sermon in Santo Domingo is the first recorded protest for indigenous rights in the history of colonization.

For four centuries, Africa supplied the Americas with manual labor and the human commodities necessary for establishing models of economic domination, and Europe benefited from the wealth produced in its overseas territories. The Africans brought by force to the Americas for this back-breaking labor had been uprooted from their cultures and families, a situation which generated endless pain and suffering. In the new, foreign land, they began to seek out and recreate spaces in which to practice their cultural and religious activities that identified them with the God who liberates. The

6. Roberto Cassá, *Historia social y económica de la República Dominicana*, vol. 1 (Santo Domingo: Alfa & Omega, 2009), 137.

enslaved black men and women never considered the God of the white man as their own. That God represented power that was not liberating, given the oppressive discourse and practices of the slave masters. Thus arose Afro-Caribbean spirituality, or popular religiosity as it is called today. The African-Brazilian theologian Silvia Regina de Lima says, "If we consider black theology through a wide lens, as the experience of God and God's different manifestations, we can say that this theology coincides with the arrival of blacks to the continent, as they brought their own religious experiences with them from Africa."[7]

Studies focusing on black presence in the DR and Latin America are few and far between, which reflects the reality of prejudice still at work in different societies within the Americas and the fact that institutions of academic research by and large pay little attention to enriching the continent through research on this subject.[8] Yet African culture in the DR is very strong and has overcome all adversities throughout history, always flowing with a spirit that resists oppression. It is apparently impossible to kill the religious and cultural richness of this population that is present and contributing to religious and social diversity all the world over.

The Catholicism brought by the Spaniards through colonization as the official religion eventually took

---

7. Silvia Regina de Lima, "La teología negra latinoamericana como un espacio de descubrimiento y afirmación del sujeto," *Pasos* 89 (May–June 2000): 41.
8. See Carlos Andújar Persinal, *Presencia negra en Santo Domingo* (Santo Domingo: Letra Gráfica, 2015).

33

root as result of the imposition the Spaniards exercised over the Tainos and the Africans. Yet Christianity in the DR drank from the enormous religious syncretism as, on its journey through history, it refused to accept Catholicism as the only religious discourse. Spanish Catholicism, especially its more somber, nuanced aspects focused on suffering, found echo and even a renewing energy in the animist practices of slaves coming from Africa. Similar to Catholicism, the Protestantism brought from the United States forcibly excluded the diverse experiences of the Dominican population and instead promoted a spirituality far removed from our daily practices. Thus, African slaves and their descendants were forced to find creative ways to continue interacting with their deities and offering them tribute. While Protestantism and Catholicism both reject these forms of belief common to the vast majority of the Dominican population, syncretistic practices are linked very strongly to the officially accepted religions which have allowed them to survive in daily life and practices.

Christianity in the DR drank from the enormous religious syncretism as it refused to accept Catholicism as the only religious discourse.

Many common beliefs and practices are characterized by this Christian-African syncretism, which is the result of the creative power of the Dominican people, the response of a new, syncretistic spirituality where different religious expressions are mixed together. Popular religiosity responds to the material and spiritual needs of the believers; it does not seek to

34

contradict or be in conflict with Catholic beliefs and practices.

Catholicism and Protestantism in the DR

As we have observed, Catholicism arrived on our island in the year 1492 through Spanish colonizers who, among other things, sought to sow the seed of Christianity and their beliefs among the native inhabitants. Regarding the endurance of Catholicism, Pablo Deiros states, "One of the most noteworthy characteristics of religious history in Latin America, before the current day, is the permanence and stability of the Roman Catholic Church. Throughout the colonial period (1492–1808), the Church brooked no challenge and remained firm in its monolithic dominance of public religion."[9] In the case of the DR, the Catholic Church maintained its control on the island for over three centuries, the only option for Christian faith among the island's inhabitants, including the indigenous and the blacks brought from Africa.

The first contact between Protestants and Hispaniola seems to have occurred around the year 1580 with the initiation of illegal trade between pirates from Holland, France, and England who brought contraband to the northwestern part of the island—today Haiti—and the inhabitants of that region.[10] As Roberto Cassá explains,

9. Pablo Deiros, *Protestantismo en América Latina ayer, hoy y mañana* (Nashville: Caribe Betania, 1997), 15.
10. See Alfonso Lockward, *Intolerancia y libertad de cultos en Santo Domingo* (Santo Domingo: DELE, 1993), 120.

35

The rise of contraband became of political interest, for the fear that it would open the floodgates of secession. The Spanish crown found particularly intolerable negotiations between its subjects and Holland, a former piece of the empire with which they were now at war. The mother country's interest, directed against both the Dutch and the inhabitants of Santo Domingo, was cloaked in religious motivation aligned with the mission of combatting Protestantism, which opposed the monarchy. There were strict consequences in place for the circulation of Protestant versions of the Bible in the black market.[11]

Protestantism was established in the DR through North American missionaries and freed blacks from the USA.

Despite these early contacts with Protestants, Protestantism was not established until much later, through North American missionaries and freed blacks who emigrated from the United States and the Lesser Antilles to the northwestern part of Hispaniola, which is now Haiti. According to Lockward, between June 1824 and July 1825, several thousand immigrants of Protestant persuasion arrived on the island, six thousand of which were free blacks from the United States. Two of these were ordained ministers in the African Methodist Episcopal Church: Reverend Scipio Beans, who moved to Port-au-Prince, and Reverend Isaac Miller, who,

36

11. Cassá, *Historia social y económica*, 198.

along with some two hundred other immigrants, was assigned to Samaná.[12] Platt traces the first Protestant worship service celebrated in Santo Domingo to 1824 with the arrival of this wave of immigrants.[13]

Both Catholicism and Protestantism have made significant contributions to the Dominican population, primarily in the areas of social aid, yet these efforts have not been generalized among the different expressions within each branch of Christianity. The Catholic Church has had a clear impact on hundreds of people through the different schools and colleges it runs under the auspices of the national department of education. Likewise, Protestant denominations like the Iglesia Evangélica Dominicana (founded jointly by the Methodist Episcopalian, Presbyterian, and United Brethren denominations from the United States in 1922), Baptists, Episcopalians, and some Pentecostal congregations also work in education through private schools. It must be recognized that for many, many years, Catholics and Protestants eyed each other as enemies, which led to difficult attitudes, a lack of respect, and a great deal of religious intolerance in the country. Yet, over time, these two spheres of the Christian faith have come to relate with an amicable spirit of cooperation. As of 2014, 57 percent of the population

12. George A. Lockward, *El Protestantismo en Dominicana* (Santo Domingo: Educativa Dominicana, 1982), 80.
13. Darío Platt, *Nueva esperanza para Santo Domingo* (Santo Domingo: Universidad Cetec,1981), 31.

self-identified as Catholic, 23 percent as Protestant, 18 percent as unaffiliated, and 2 percent as "other."[14]

Current Christian Realities in the DR: Challenges

Our long walk through the history of our country and Christianity in the DR has shown us Christianity divided between two great branches, Catholicism and Protestantism, both of which have sown light and darkness in their religious, educational, and social work among our people. From the start, both groups were motivated by particular interests that benefitted their leaders in Spain or in the United States. Few groups in the two spheres have shown genuine interest in the social aspects of the gospel of Jesus Christ. The motivations of the institutions that came earliest to Dominican territory were far from centered on preaching a liberating message. A cursory look at our country's history shows that from the start, Christianity was imposed by force. It was not chosen freely by the Tainos and black slaves, and Protestantism often spread through tactics of forcible cultural persuasion.

Few Catholic or Protestant groups have shown genuine interest in the social aspects of the gospel of Jesus Christ.

14. Pew Research, "Religion in Latin America: Widespread Change in a Historically Catholic Region," November 13, 2014, https://www.pewforum.org/2014/11/13/religion-in-latin-america.

The reality of Christianity today in our country has undergone changes as new challenges come over time, and the Christian faith is called to face the changes. Day after day, more and more people come seeking a message of faith and hope. This is how Christianity remains viable and relevant for the DR in the twenty-first century. Religious institutions are still generally respected by the government and society. This is a point in their favor for continuing to carry out the divine mission incarnated in Jesus of Nazareth, who lived and walked among us and showed that a life pleasing to God is based on love and unconditional service to the most vulnerable, the "least of these."

We must also recognize that the Christianity that has developed in our country tends to be very conservative. It has not spearheaded great social change or supported grassroots ecclesial communities as has occurred in other countries. When there is openness to a liberating Christianity, as seen in the liberation theologies of the 1970s, it generally occurs within academia and the upper echelons of denominational or Catholic leadership. There is a disconnect between those who are open to the immediate social ramifications of the gospel and the masses practicing the faith day by day.

We will conclude our review of Christianity within the DR by discussing some of the principle challenges it faces:

There is a disconnect between those who are open to the immediate social ramifications of the gospel and the masses practicing the faith day by day.

39

- greater biblical, theological, exegetical, and hermeneutical formation for followers of Christianity;

- sincere, honest dialogue between biblical/theological sciences and social sciences;

- interreligious dialogue between the various religious expressions present in the DR, including Christianity, African and indigenous spiritualities, Judaism, Islam, and other religions from India that have recently begun to spread;

- thorough development of theology and practices regarding the relationship of the church and politics, as increasingly more Christians get involved in the country's political life and aspire to run for public office;

- promotion of a Jesus who walks closely with those who suffer, a human Jesus who identifies with and relates to real people as he did with the Samaritan woman;

- caring for creation, remembering that God's command places humanity in a role of caretaking, not abuse and exploitation as is the case today;

- interfaith dialogue between Catholics and Protestants to help face the country's current problems;

- breaking with the historic conservatism that has closely linked Christianity with the most entrenched, unyielding spheres of power in the political, cultural, and religious realms;

- deepening our social commitment, reorienting our perspective from denominational positions or credal preferences to adopt the perspective of Jesus of Nazareth who showed concern for the social outcasts of his day;

- promoting equal opportunities for men and women, supporting the formation of female leaders and treating them with the same respect and approval as male leaders;

- fighting against every kind of discrimination, shaking off prejudices and respecting diverse expressions of sexuality;

- developing plans and strategies of inclusion so that churches are spaces where people of different physical and mental capabilities are able to freely engage in the Christian faith: for example, the deaf community, or those in wheelchairs (currently only a very few churches have wheelchair-accessible ramps);

- ceasing to view children as objects and instead considering children as subjects with rights in communities of faith, based on Jesus's relationship with children as the example for participating in the kingdom of heaven;

41

- and helping establish genuine religious pluralism in the DR in which all faiths are committed to building a culture of peace and social well-being.

The Church in Panama: An Open Field of Opportunities

Marina Medina Moreno

The State of the Nation

Panama, a small country of around 29,000 square miles and some 4.3 million inhabitants,[1] is the isthmus where Central America meets South America. Mountains, plains, and beautiful beaches stretch over its territory, only interrupted by the basin of the Panama Canal. This famous feat of human engineering

---

1. World Population Review, "Panama Population 2020," updated August 27, 2019, http://worldpopulationreview.com/countries/panama-population/.

Marina Medina Moreno, from Panama, is a Sub-Regional Coordinator for Latin America for IFES. She lives in Panama and provides training, support, and leadership development for every IFES-related student movement in the region. In the past she served as the coordinator for the Panama chapter of the FTL.

43

cuts the country in half and joins the Atlantic and Pacific Oceans to create an essential sea route.

Panama's position as a throughway turned the country early on into a crossroads for cultures from around the world. Seventy percent of the population is mestizo, that is, the descendants of European and indigenous natives. Around 14 percent is a different kind of mestizo: the descendants of indigenous natives and Africans who either were forcibly brought to Panama as slaves or who migrated from the Caribbean to build the railroads and later the canal. In the mix are also the descendants of Asians who came to build the railroads. Around 10 percent are white, and the remaining 6 percent are direct descendants of the original people groups living in the region when white colonists arrived. Altogether, over 12 percent of the population is indigenous,[2] representing several different original people groups.[3]

Panama's position as a throughway has turned the country into a crossroads for cultures from around the world.

According to its constitution, Panama's government is a united, democratic, representative republic in which the different state bodies work in concert with the president. In the most recent elections, held May 5, 2019, Laurentino Cortizo was elected president. The leaders from the past decade have left the country in a morass of corruption and economic slowdown, greatly widening the gap between the extremely wealthy and the desperately poor. The current president

---

2. "Indigenous" refers to the original people groups living on the land when European colonizers arrived, and to their descendants.
3. World Population Review, "Panama Population 2020."

faces enormous, urgent challenges for improving the country.

Even so, economic experts and international bodies have declared that Panama is "one of the fastest growing economies in the world," and the "second fastest growing economy in Latin America and the Caribbean."[4] This situation provides security for investors and attracts the gaze of the larger world powers. Yet this positive situation does not translate into improved quality of life for most Panamanians. Poverty levels hover at 14 percent and extreme poverty around 6.6 percent, the brunt of which falls on the shoulders of indigenous populations living in rural areas.[5]

There is much to celebrate about the current reality of Panama: there are options for employment, the country has continued modernizing over time, and there is openness to and respect for our indigenous population. We rejoice that, while prejudice certainly exists in our country which is a crucible of so many ethnicities, there is little room for the rampant discrimination so common in other nations.

This positive economic situation does not translate into improved quality of life for most Panamanians.

Even so, we recognize that the quality of our health care must be improved. All wage earners pay into the health care system, yet quality of care is not equal in all regions. The health care system is fragmented such

4. The World Bank, "The World Bank in Panama: Overview," updated October 10, 2019, https://www.worldbank.org/en/country/panama/overview.
5. Ibid.

that it places an undue burden on users, who must secure separate appointments for each step of the process and may not even be able to acquire the medicine they are eventually prescribed. The unwieldy system pushes many to overuse hospital emergency rooms where all parts of an evaluation can occur in one day in one place, and patients are more likely to walk away with the necessary medicines.[6] Alejandra Carrillo, an analyst for the Panamanian branch of the Pan American Health Organization, comments on the fragmented nature of Panama's healthcare system and states that it "reinforces inequalities in care" according to demographics.[7]

Public education in Panama is also begging for reform and improvement. While free schooling is available to all children and Panama boasts impressive literacy rates in its official statistics,[8] the quality of the education and the educational structures desperately need attention. There is vast disparity in the quality of private versus public education, as well as disparity in the quality of public education between regions. Official statistics can gild over on-the-ground reality.

Health care and public education in Panama are begging for reform.

---

6. Enrique Lau Cortés, "¿Hacia dónde va la salud en Panamá?" *La Prensa*, December 4, 2017, https://www.prensa.com/opinion/va-salud-Panama_0_4909759080.html.
7. Organización Panamericana de la Salud, "¿Cómo mejorar la calidad de los Centros de Salud?" September 25, 2018, https://www.paho.org/pan/index.php?option=com_content&view=article&id=1115:como-mejorar-la-calidad-de-los-centros-de-salud&Itemid=442.
8. It is projected that, by 2020, the illiteracy rate in the country will be well below 3 percent. Ministerio de Desarrollo Social, "Más de 76 mil jóvenes y adultos han aprendido a leer y escribir en la última década," September 10, 2019, https://www.mides.gob.pa/mas-de-76-mil-jovenes-y-adultos-han-aprendido-a-leer-y-escribir-en-panama/.

Despite a literacy rate of around 95 percent, Panama ranks near the bottom of the list of seventy-seven countries evaluated for educational progress by the Organisation for Economic Co-operation and Development. The OECD found that more than six out of every ten students fifteen years of age cannot read a text and understand what it means. The evaluations in science and math are even worse.[9] It is clear that the public education available to Panamanian students is not equipping them with basic skills.

Another reality that Panama faces, like most countries in our region, is the enormous challenge of immigration. An estimated 25,000 people trek through the Darién each year en route from Asia, Africa, South America, and Cuba toward the United States; countless others never make it out. These migrants represent everything from the desperate situation of children attempting to be reunited with their parents to rings of drug and human trafficking.[10] In the midst of their desperation, we can celebrate that the reality of migration has been reflected in the church. Many churches have become centers of aid for migrants, offering support and hope.

Many churches have become centers of aid for migrants.

9. Victoria Isabel Cardiel C., "La educación panameña ocupa los últimos puestos, según resultados de la prueba PISA," *La Prensa*, December 3, 2019, https://www.prensa.com/mundo/la-educacion-panamena-ocupa-los-ultimos-puestos-segun-pisa/.
10. La Liga Contra el Silencio, "El Darién: La frontera de los migrantes invisibles," Cerosetenta, November 13, 2018, https://cerosetenta.uniandes.edu.co/el-darien-inmigrantes/.

47

The State of the Church

As in most of Latin America, Catholicism is the majority religion in Panama, a fact which is recognized in the constitution even while the laws guarantee freedom of religion. Protestant Christians make up about 20 percent of the total population.[11] Just as Panama is

Protestant Christians make up about 20 percent of the total population.

an amalgamation of cultures, it is also a melting pot of Christian traditions and denominations. There are few studies and scarce demographic data regarding the particular makeup of Protestantism in Panama. Clifton Holland is one who has documented the presence of mainline denominations, smaller Protestant denominations, and myriad Pentecostal denominations. In his 2001 "Historical Profile of Religion in Panama," he notes that, "In 1980, the largest Protestant denominations in Panama were the Foursquare Church, the Episcopal Church, the Adventist Church, and the Baptist Convention. However, by 2000, the Assemblies of God had become the largest denomination in Panama as a result of 20-years of strenuous evangelistic and church-planting efforts throughout the country."[12] With at least six Pentecostal megachurches,[13] it is safe to

---

11. It was 19 percent as of 2014, according to the Pew Research Center. See Pew Research, "Religion in Latin America: Widespread Change in a Historically Catholic Region," November 13, 2014, https://www.pewforum.org/2014/11/13/religion-in-latin-america.
12. Clifton L. Holland, "Historical Profile of Religion in Panama," The Latin American Socio-Religious Studies Program (PROLADES), rev. July 20, 2001, http://www.prolades.com/religion/panama.html.
13. See "Protestant Mega-Churches in Panama," PROLADES, 2012, http://www.prolades.com/cra/regions/cam/megachurches_pan.htm.

conclude that Panama follows the wider trend throughout Latin America of Protestantism being made up in its majority (65 percent as of 2014) by Pentecostals.[14]

Positive Aspects

In recent years, the Protestant evangelical church has come to better understand its role in engaging the country's social realities. Many churches run centers that provide meals for children; safe homes for abandoned children or the elderly (like Hogar el Milagro of the Foursquare Church and Juntos Podemos, which provides academic scholarships for children from poor areas); programs that help the indigent (like Comida para la Calle from the Casa de Oración Christian Church); and rigorous programs of rehabilitation in the country's jails (like Rema and Viniste a Mí). Ministries dedicated to strengthening marriages (like Vínculos para el Cambio), supporting parents, and combatting child abuse have sprung up throughout the country. Social service programs like these are not limited to the Protestant sector. The Catholic Church is also heavily involved in all of these realms.

Challenges for the Church

More than an organization, the church is a body, the dwelling of the Holy Spirit. As such, the church is responsible for promoting the values of the kingdom of

49

---

14. Pew Research, "Religion in Latin America."

God in all areas of life, from personal and private realms to communal and public spheres.

The church has paid little attention to artistic expression.

In this regard, the church in Panama has fallen far short in several key areas. It has paid little attention to artistic expression, neither redeeming art from the larger culture in such a way that exalts Christ nor equipping artists who follow Jesus to utilize their gifts according to a consistent Christian ethic. And it has shown little leadership or interest in caring for the environment. Nor has the church adequately faced rogue groups that claim to be Christians but who have twisted the Scriptures and preach something other than a gospel of grace: versions of prosperity gospel. Sadly, these distortions are all too common.

Examples of Faithful Obedience to God in Public Spaces

The general disposition is to not involve the church directly in partisan politics.

One example of the church in Panama's obedience to God is the general disposition to not involve the church directly in partisan politics, though individuals are free to engage as they see fit, and many form alliances to exercise political pressure based on their evangelical values. In other countries in our region, the formation of specifically evangelical political parties has been rife with conflict and generally has not been an avenue for demonstrating what it means to follow Jesus. The different denominations in Panama have handled this issue soberly. If brothers or sisters in the faith desire to run for a particular office, their local church will generally bless and support them emotionally and spiritually; yet their political work is carried out from within a political party, independent of church involvement. There have been attempts to form evangelical-based political parties, like the MAR-PAIS party in 2017, but as yet none have gained enough traction to put forth a candidate in general elections. Experiences in other countries in our region indicate that this is likely for the best. Commenting in 2017, Claire Nevache explains it this way:

> While evangelicals are without a doubt involved in politics, we cannot consider the evangelicals of Panama as a homogenous actor, since they lack a common strategy and have no determined methodology for resolving differences and conflicts. However, the MAR-PAIS party [est. 2017], which is unarguably based on the influence of evangelicals on the whole—and this despite the opposition of some evangelicals to the project of a political party—does constitute a new entry into politics on the part of evangelicals.[15]

---

15. Claire Nevache, "Las iglesias evangélicas en Panamá: Análisis de la emergencia de un nuevo actor político," (paper presented at the 9th Latin American Congress of Political Science, organized by the Asociación Lationamericana de Ciencia Política; Montevideo, July 26–28, 2019), 29, http://www.congresoalacip2017.org/arquivo/download public2?q=YToyOntzOjY6InBhcmFtcyI7czozNToiYToxOntzOjEwOiJJRF9B UlFVSVZPIjtzOjQ6IjI0MzciO30iO3M6MToiaCI7czozMjoiY2QwZmQ5MGFmYzA0M mIwZTdmNWFhNTVjZTdhNjllZTki030%3D.

Another example of the church's involvement in the public sphere was the alliance of evangelicals and Catholics that came together and offered alternatives to the legislative assembly's plan for sex education. This alliance included teachers, medical personnel, and representatives of other fields as well. Since 2014, the government has considered a bill called Proyecto 61 regarding sex education in the public schools. The bill is a desperately needed attempt to respond to the serious problems of teen pregnancies and sexually transmitted diseases, among other matters. While the bill garnered support among various sectors of society, this coalition of Protestant and Catholic churches collaborated to help edit articles that concerned them and write alternative articles for the bill under consideration. Proyecto 61 and the extreme reactions it has elicited have, on the one hand, marked stark contrasts in ideological understandings of appropriate political activity for Christians; and, on the other, have been an opportunity for the church to seek dialogue and cooperation across ideological lines regarding an issue so key for the well-being of the nation's citizenry, especially young people. With government turnover, the processes remain ongoing, as Proyecto 61 has not yet advanced toward implementation.

In its proclamation of the gospel, the Panamanian church has been aware of its location within a throughway country and its ethnic diversity. Throughout its history, Panama has been considered a melting pot of races and now of ethnicities. Panama is host to a variety of communities and ethnicities, including various communities of blacks, indigenous, Jews, and people from China, India, Spain, and other countries. The mixture of ethnicities has created the group of mulattos and mestizos that populate Panama today. At the same time, Panama is also a throughway country, attracting migrants of many different nationalities. Because of these demographic realities, churches in Panama have historically gathered together people of various different ethnicities in one place. There is no doubt that the Panamanian church is multicultural. The church today is rich in cultural diversity not only as a reflection of the ethnic groups within it but also of the diverse subcultures that make up the unique Panamanian identity.

There is no doubt that the Panamanian church is multicultural.

Over the years I personally have seen how the church has grown, how brothers and sisters from the spectrum of sectors in Panama get involved in this crucible of colors and social statuses and thus experience the interethnic nature of cultural diversity.

Voices from and to the Worldwide Church

In the midst of some encouraging signs of the church in Panama growing in faithful obedience to God, many pastors preach a theology misaligned with the gospel of the kingdom of God. Sadly, a health and wealth gospel, which promises physical well-being and material comforts in a transactional exchange for obeying God

53

and his ministers, is the daily bread of many churches. This distortion promotes a faith at odds with the Word of God. Thus, the church in Panama needs to learn how to work together in unity; how to develop and live out a theology of the kingdom of God in which the church simultaneously preaches the gospel and practices holistic mission.

Our Panamanian churches need to let go of the frenzy for activity and learn to focus on the formation of disciples who follow Christ. These lessons can be learned from our brothers and sisters around the world and also from others right here in Panama. Certain parachurch ministries, like the Panamanian student movement associated with the International Fellowship of Evangelical Students, have a wealth of experience and knowledge at the church's disposal. Many of these ministries are serious about their commitment to mission, the Word, and discipleship, and the church would greatly benefit from their example.

Our Panamanian churches need to let go of the frenzy for activity and learn to focus on the formation of disciples.

In a way, the realities faced by the church in Panama are indicative of the realities faced by the church throughout Latin America and perhaps beyond. Panama is not the only country in need of a call to repentance, to unity, to returning to God's Word, and to embracing the good news of God's kingdom. The church's mission must always revolve around Jesus, be connected to the Word of God, be proclaimed verbally, and be lived out practically moment by moment.

Indigenous Communities in Panama: Brief Reflections on Ancestral Memory and Creation

Jocabed Reina Solano Miselis

The indigenous peoples of Abya Yala[1] in Panama have lived in the territories for hundreds of years. The indigenous nations that fall within the more recent

---

1. "Abya Yala" is the term used by the Gunadule people to refer to what is commonly called Latin America.

Jocabed Reina Solano Miselis, from the Gunadule people in the Guna Yala region in Panama, has a degree in tourism administration and is working on her master's of theology through the Center for Interdisciplinary Theological Studies (CETI). The codirector of Memoria Indígena, she works among indigenous peoples with the intersections of identity, faith, and culture. She also coordinates the FTL's group on identity, indigeneity, and interculturality.

55

territorial designation of Panama include the Gunadule, Emberá, Wounaan, Buglé, Ngäbe, Naso, and Bri Bri. With their strength, knowledge, work, art, food sources, resistance, and insurrection, they have marked their path in this country. The path has not been easy; it has come at the high cost of the lives of thousands of indigenous brothers and sisters. Their cosmogony, based on spirituality nurtured by an understanding of the land and our relationship to it, has given us a country that has set aside areas for conservation. For example, in 1981, the Darién region of Panama was declared a UNESCO World Heritage Site and in 1983 was named a World Biosphere Reserve. A great biodiversity of plants, trees, and animals is conserved in indigenous territories. This biodiversity encompasses plant genes, seeds, and wisdom that contribute to the life and heart of what Panama is but which so often goes unrecognized by the Panamanian mestizos who are out of touch with the memories of the people groups whose struggle to survive is informed by their indigenous identity.

A great biodiversity of plants, trees, and animals is conserved in indigenous territories.

Panama's indigenous communities have been tending to, preserving, and relating to the land with love and respect for centuries. Yet our Christian churches throughout Panama demonstrate a malnourished theology of creation. Preserving the biodiversity of our plants, trees, animals, and the birds that migrate to Panama every year should flow out of a robust theology of what abundant life means. This abundant life shows us we are part of creation and thus allows us

56

to incarnate our vocation as responsible caretakers of what God has made.[2]

The church in Panama has the challenging opportunity to follow Jesus's model of embrace, hospitality, justice, and active compassion in so many realms. In this endeavor, the church would greatly benefit from listening to our indigenous communities. While there is diversity between indigenous communities and practices in Panama, indigenous groups generally offer a holistic understanding of community in terms of social and cosmic milieu. That is, all living beings are mutually interdependent. This concept offers a way of approaching social relationships that is in stark contrast to the capitalistic modes that dominate relationships in the globalized world today: modes marked by utilitarianism, individualism, consumerism, patriarchy, and ruthless competition. Sadly, these same traits are all too apparent within the Panamanian Christian church. Indigenous voices hold out a way of understanding the encounters between cultures (or between any subject and an "other") that is not based on a colonial mindset. Instead, indigenous cultures generally reflect the New Testament commitment to life together in a way that values plurality and diversity.

> *The church would greatly benefit from listening to our indigenous communities.*

---

2. See Ruth Padilla Deborst, "Jardinería planetaria: Memoria indígena y escatología subversiva," unpublished paper presented at the Asociación Educativa Teológica Evangélica (AETE) Conference, "Palabra de Dios, Escatología y Política en América Latina," November 14–17, 2018.

57

Learning from the convergence of the various people groups living in Panama—including indigenous communities, Chinese, Indians, Italians, Jews, Venezuelans, Colombians, Nicaraguans, Spaniards, Greeks, US Americans, peoples of African descent, mestizos, and others—compels us in the Christian faith to work together on intercultural projects that build bridges of reconciliation, life, and justice in Panama. The church in Panama could offer so much if it began to work from a place of mutual epistemological respect and wisdom[3] and in favor of society's disadvantaged members. The church could articulate, create, and be involved in public policies that nurture a thriving life together in the country. Evangelicals have the opportunity to offer grounded, interdisciplinary, and practical proposals for the grievous problems our country faces. Thus they could participate in Jesus's narrative of reconciliation through extending his love and abundant life to all his creation.

---

3. As one author says, "Epistemology talks 'about' life, wisdom speaks 'from' life." See Edgar Patricio Guerrero Arias, *La Chakana del corazonar: Desde las espiritualidades y las sabidurías insurgentes de Abya Yala* (Quito: Abya Yala, 2018), 110.

Indigenous Evangelicals in the October 2019 Uprising: A New Face for Holistic Mission in Ecuador

Rodrigo Riffo

Introduction

The goal of this brief essay is to document the role played by an association of indigenous evangelicals in the most significant indigenous uprising in Ecuadorian political life in recent years. It is often thought that

Rodrigo Riffo, from Argentina, studied biblical sciences at the Universidad Bíblica Latinoamericana in Costa Rica and has a degree in social anthropology. Currently living in Ecuador, he is an exegetical consultant for the sign language Bible translation for the hearing impaired sponsored by the United Bible Societies in Ecuador and is active in the Quito chapter of the FTL.

59

evangelical churches align themselves with whoever wields political power at any given moment. Others observe that evangelicals alienate themselves from the sociopolitical scene altogether by living a decontextualized spirituality. There are numerous examples that give credence to each of these opinions. Yet the case addressed in this essay presents an evangelical association that actively participated in the struggle against austerity measures imposed by President Lenín Moreno which would have had a disproportionately negative impact on the poorest sectors of society. After setting the scene and describing the activity of the aforementioned evangelical association, this essay will conclude with a series of challenges for the mission of the church today.

The State of the Nation

Ecuador is a relatively small nation on the northwest Pacific coast of South America. Stretching over some 109,000 square miles, the country is divided into three primary regions: the coastal plains, the mountainous Andean region, and the eastern region. Famous for its geographic location along the equator, the nation is also renowned for the Galapagos Islands which played a role in the development of Darwin's theories of evolutionary biology. Precolonial history can be traced archeologically back to 3000 BC, and the land was populated by various people groups that were conquered by the Inca empire in the late AD 1400s. The

Spaniards arrived in the 1500s, imposing both Spanish culture and Roman Catholicism and either decimating or enslaving the native inhabitants, as well as importing slaves from Africa. After independence in 1822, Ecuador was part of Gran Colombia until 1830 when it became an independent republic. Since then, the nation has experienced nearly constant social, economic, and political upheaval, marked by pockets of dictatorial rule and occasional seasons of prosperity and social progress.[1] The country's estimated 17.5 million inhabitants are a mixture of mestizos (descendants of Spanish colonists and indigenous peoples), whites of European descent, descendants of black slaves, and indigenous descendants of the original people groups (around 7 percent of the population).[2] There are numerous indigenous groups in Ecuador, each with their own culture and language, or sometimes sharing the Quichua language, which was an enduring legacy of the Inca empire.[3]

Indigenous descendants of the original people groups make up around 7 percent of the population.

1. Data summarized from Homero Pozo Vélez, Murdo J. MacLeod, and Gregory W. Knapp, "Ecuador," *Encyclopaedia Britannica*, last updated November 1, 2019, https://www.britannica.com/place/Ecuador; and World Population Review, "Ecuador Population 2020," updated February 17, 2020, https://worldpopulationreview.com/countries/ecuador-population/.
2. See Instituto Nacional de Estadística y Censos, "Resultados del Censo 2010," https://www.ecuadorencifras.gob.ec/resultados/.
3. See Sistema Integrado de Indicadores Sociales del Ecuador, "Listado de nacionalidades y pueblos indígenas del Ecuador," http://www.siise.gob.ec/siiseweb/PageWebs/glosario/ficglo_napuin.htm.

61

The Crisis of October 2019

Lenín Moreno became president of the Republic of Ecuador on May 24, 2017. Previously, he had served as vice president during the first term of Rafael Correa's populist administration. As Correa was finishing his second term under the new constitution, Lenín Moreno was the Alianza País presidential candidate in the 2017 general elections, representing the vast working-class wing of the electorate. At that time, Moreno's main competitor was Guillermo Lasso, a wealthy bank director who represented the interests of multinational corporations and the classic far-right discourse of progress, development, and participation in the international market. Moreno beat Lasso in a run-off, in an atmosphere clouded by doubts stemming from accusations of electoral fraud. The difference between Moreno and Lasso was slight, less than 3 percent of the voting roll. These extremely close results demonstrated the social schism between those who wanted to continue the populist policies begun by Rafael Correa and those who were weary of all the corruption and were opposed to high government spending. Regardless of the narrow margin between them, the direct popular vote declares the winner, and in that election, Ecuador decided to support Lenín Moreno and to continue the trajectory of prioritizing social welfare above the interests of large corporations.

When he took office, Moreno committed to take no actions that would negatively impact the most vulnerable members of society.[4] Yet two years later, on October 2, 2019, President Moreno eliminated, among other measures, the subsidies for gasoline and diesel through Decree 883, which subsequently increased the costs related to transportation and food. Ecuador's citizenry interpreted this decree to be a betrayal of the people. It did not help the political situation that the International Monetary Fund (IMF) was the organization pushing these measures of reducing governmental expenditures. The IMF's equation is always the same for underdeveloped countries in debt: reduce public spending to balance the budget. At that time, one option to stabilize the country's fiscal situation could have been budgetary investments to stimulate industry and thus increase productivity. But, no, the option that the government chose, under the guidance of the IMF, was to reduce public spending, as is so often the case among governments pressured by the IMF. To put it bluntly, reducing public spending actually means reducing the percentage of the budget that the state directs toward society's most vulnerable members.

Ecuador's citizenry interpreted Decree 883 to be a betrayal of the people.

Public discontent was not slow in coming. On October 4, 2019, the public transportation industry initiated a forty-eight-hour national strike. Unrest among public transportation workers and their determination

---

4. See his inauguration speech. Presidencia República del Ecuador, "Discurso de posesión del Presidente Lenín Moreno Garcés" (May 24, 2017), 6, https://www.presidencia.gob.ec/wp-content/uploads/downloads/2017/06/2017.05.24-DISCURSO-POSESI%C3%93N-ANTE-LA-ASAMBLEA-NACIONAL.pdf.

63

to insist on repealing Decree 883 kicked off hotspots of protest and violence throughout the country. Several unions quickly joined the strike. Yet, by October 7, an association of indigenous groups was at the helm of the protests. These actors had not had such strong and vehement public presence since 1990, when indigenous groups rose up to demand land rights, basic services like running water, the recognition of ancestral medicine, and intercultural, bilingual education.

Indigenous groups from different provinces of the country started a memorable trek to Quito, the nation's capital. Some legs of the journey were made on foot while the marchers chanted the famous chorus, "El pueblo, unido, ¡jamás será vencido!" ("United, the people will never be defeated!"). Other legs of the difficult journey were made by truck and bus. Ecuador's army attempted to halt the advance of the indigenous onslaught through repression. Yet their mission failed to contain the mobilizations given the number of indigenous groups coming from every nook and cranny of the country. An estimated 20,000 indigenous people descended upon the capital. As they journeyed toward the center of Quito, the multitude was spurred on by cheers and applause from many of Quito's inhabitants who turned out to receive the marchers like war heroes. The political impact of the indigenous masses that swept through the nation's capital was so great that President Moreno and his ministers fled to the coastal city of Guayaquil and

An estimated 20,000 indigenous people descended upon the capital.

decreed that the seat of government had been changed to that city, out of caution.

From Guayaquil, the government refused to bend to pressure. It sent the army out to the streets and brutally repressed the protests. Supported by the strong arm of media power, the government combatted the indigenous groups both physically—around fifteen indigenous men and women died as a result of the repression, and thousands were injured—and symbolically, as the government endeavored alongside mass media to persuade the Ecuadorian population that the presence of the indigenous groups in Quito posed a national threat. Social tension skyrocketed. Food and fuel shortages heightened the conflict. Schools, workplaces, social events, and basically all activities in the country were paralyzed for the twelve days of protest.

Throughout this time, the indigenous movements—including men, women, and children—were housed by entities that opened their doors in solidarity and supported the popular outcry. These places of asylum were mainly Catholic universities, the Universidad Central (the capital's largest public university), and the Casa de la Cultura (House of Culture, which oversees the country's libraries and museums, among other things). These locations also served as hubs for the donations that Quito's society sent to sustain the protest. These peaceful places were key points of medical attention for those wounded in the protests. On several occasions, the military and police attacked these refuges,

65

endangering the lives of those within regardless of age or gender.

Finally, with the intervention and mediation of the United Nations and the Ecuadorian Conference of Catholic Bishops, the government entered into dialogue with indigenous leaders. After several hours of discussion and debate, Lenín Moreno agreed to repeal Decree 883. With that decision, the indigenous communities returned to their respective provinces, and life in Ecuador resumed its normal rhythms. Gasoline and diesel returned to their subsidized prices, and food and transportation costs did not rise. The problem of an imbalanced budget remains and has yet to be resolved by the government; yet the victory achieved by the indigenous movement, supported by Quito's inhabitants, significantly benefitted every sector in Ecuador.

The victory achieved by the indigenous movement significantly benefitted every sector in Ecuador.

The State of the Church

Before discussing the role of evangelicals in the indigenous protests of October 2019, a brief sketch of the religious landscape of the country is in order. The Roman Catholic hold over Ecuador persisted nearly unbroken until the Liberal Revolution of 1895, after which Protestant missions, denominations, and missionary agencies entered the country.[5] Not until the Constitution of 1906 were church and state separated, yet the Catholic Church retained certain privileges. The massive incursion of Protestantism began in the 1950s in Ecuador.[6] As Julián Guamán observes, "In Ecuador, the missionaries were not so much *Protestants* (mainline-classical) but rather mainly *evangelical* (from the evangelical line). They had no intention of becoming part of the social fabric but were just passing through on a mission of evangelization."[7] The denominational spectrum in Ecuador today mirrors the scene in the United States. By and large, mainline denominations appeal to the upper and middle classes and are committed to civil and social rights; evangelical Protestants tend to be moderate (pietist) or fundamentalist and are common in indigenous communities and poor urban neighborhoods, emphasizing legalistic ethics and simplistic doctrines; and Pentecostal churches, with their emphasis on speaking in tongues, healings, and exorcisms, are strongest in the poorest sectors of the country.[8] Currently, Protestants account for between 11 and 13 percent of the population, while Catholics are 79

> *Evangelical missionaries 'had no intention of becoming part of the social fabric but were just passing through.'*

---

5. Julián Guamán, "Protestantismo en el Ecuador: Tipología y formas institucionales" (unpublished draft, Quito, 2010), 16, http://www.prolades.com/cra/regions/sam/ecu/Protestantismo_en_Ecuador_Guaman_2010.pdf. Later published as *Evangélicos en el Ecuador: Tipologías y formas institucionales del protestantismo* (Quito: Abya Yala, 2011).
6. Ibid.
7. Ibid., 19.
8. Julián Guamán, "Panorama de la *Iglesia Evangélica* en el Ecuador," (unpublished paper, 2008), 2–4, http://www.prolades.com/cra/regions/sam/ecu/panorama_iglesia_evangelica_ecuador_2008_guaman.pdf.

percent, and the rest are either unaffiliated or belong to minority religions.[9]

The case of indigenous evangelicals is slightly different from the trajectory of Protestantism in the rest of the country. Guamán observes that, "Though evangelized by several fundamentalist evangelical missions and churches, these offshoots have gone through a process of self-definition and have developed more than five hundred local congregations of their own throughout the country."[10] The Consejo de Pueblos y Organizaciones Indígenas Evangélicas del Ecuador (FEINE, Council of Evangelical Indigenous Peoples and Organizations of Ecuador), founded in 1980, brings many of these indigenous evangelical believers together.

The Role of the Church in the Socioeconomic Conflict

As we have seen, there are many different evangelical churches in Latin America. A simplistic approach to the diverse manifestations of evangelicalism does not allow a thorough understanding of churches' different reactions to situations of economic and social upheaval. The varying ways that churches responded to the crisis in October 2019 is a case in point. Evangelical churches are as different as they

---

9. Pew Research, "Religion in Latin America: Widespread Change in a Historically Catholic Region," November 13, 2014, https://www.pewforum.org/2014/11/13/religion-in-latin-america; and World Population Review, "Ecuador Population 2020."
10. Guamán, "Panorama," 3.

are complex in their public spheres. Even so, we can observe that, faced with the October 2019 social crisis, the positions adopted by evangelical churches oscillated between "seeking peace" on the one hand and "seeking justice" on the other. These opposing postures reflect two antagonistic understandings of God, and there is biblical support for both divine models.

The first posture, adopted primarily by various middle-class evangelical churches—which generally seek to maintain their social status and to live in relative comfort and safety—is rooted in the idea that God calls us to peace and reconciliation. Along these lines, God abhors violence and the lack of dialogue, and God calls brothers and sisters to love and forgive each other. The second posture, adopted by other evangelical churches, is an activist stance. For this group, God is a political being who wants justice for the most vulnerable and will not rest until God's kingdom comes in all its fullness. For these churches, God is angry and abhors injustice.

FEINE falls within this latter camp. This organization, under its president, the pastor Eustaquio Tuala, joined the indigenous protest, thus highlighting two fundamental aspects of its identity. First, they are indigenous groups and, thus, are aligned with the work of all indigenous movements. Second, they are evangelicals, and their reading of the Bible urges them to fight on behalf of society's most vulnerable members in harmony with the kingdom of God.

69

For this reason, around 700 people associated with FEINE, including indigenous evangelical pastors and leaders, traveled among the multitudinous caravans toward Quito, to present their complaints and demand the repeal of Decree 883. These protesters were housed in the main headquarters of FEINE. Many evangelical churches in Quito aided FEINE with food and hygiene items, as well as gauze, alcohol, and other medical supplies for tending to those wounded by police repression. During the protest, the police detained pastor Eustaquio Tuala along with several social leaders, under accusations of disturbing the peace. Pastor Tuala was released within days, and, as he left the commissary, he encouraged FEINE's evangelicals to continue their nonviolent resistance. Among the evangelicals involved in the protest, there were no acts of violence in their demonstrations. On the contrary, the evangelical indigenous group repeatedly paused in the midst of the protest to kneel and pray, begging God for justice. Even so, the consistent police response was excessive repression, which is why the participation of evangelicals within the indigenous protest registers deaths at the hands of police force. Such is the case of our brother in the faith Edgar Yucailla, who died due to a head injury inflicted by firearms.[11] At a gathering held by the Quito chapter of the Fraternidad Teológica Latinoamericana (FTL; Latin

> Among the evangelicals involved in the protest, there were no acts of violence in their demonstrations.

---

11. "El dirigente indígena Edgar Yucailla fue herido en la cabeza el 12 de octubre; murió tras convalecer 17 días en Quito," *El Comercio*, November 1, 2019, https://www.elcomercio.com/actualidad/edgar-yucailla-guamote-protestas-muerte.html.

American Theological Fellowship), the pastor Samuel Lema, an indigenous leader in FEINE, stated that, for those involved in FEINE, being evangelical means respecting the memory of those who gave their lives for a just cause.[12]

On October 13, 2019, in the negotiations mediated by the UN and the Catholic Church, Eustaquio Tuala was seated next to President Moreno. Pastor Tuala's words were decisive and rang with biblical radicalism. "There can be no peace if there is no justice," he said, echoing Isaiah 32:17, "The fruit of that righteousness [justice][13] will be peace; its effect will be quietness and confidence forever."

Challenges for the Church

It seems that, in Ecuador, those who advocate for a God of peace and love are speaking from within a privileged social and economic status they do not want to lose. In this sense, "peace" is a social calm that the middle class needs in order to feel safe and secure. Meanwhile, those who work in solidarity for justice (Mic 6:8) generally find themselves in an unfavorable social

Indigenous communities are subjects of the mission of God.

---

12. This gathering, titled "Evangelical Churches in the Socioeconomic Reality of Ecuador," was held on October 24, 2019.

13. The Hebrew word *tsedeq* is most often translated "righteousness" in English versions of the Bible, yet it is rendered as *justicia* ("justice") in most Spanish versions of the Bible. See Steven Voth, "Justice vs. Righteousness: A Contextualized Analysis of 'tsedeq' in the KJV (English) and RVR (Spanish)," *Journal of Biblical Text Research* (Korean Bible Societies) 20 (April 2007): 279–310, https://www.bskorea.or.kr/data/pdf/20-13%20Justice%20vs.%20Righteousness%20A%20Contextualized%20Analysis%20(Steven%20Voth).pdf.

71

position. Is it possible to reconcile peace and justice? Will peace ever be the fruit of justice? This is the primary challenge that the evangelical faith faces: that is, accepting only the peace that springs from justice, and understanding justice as true dignity for all that God has created. In 1992, FEINE signed the "Otavalo Declaration," ratified at the Third Latin American Congress on Evangelization (CLADE III). Resolution 8 of that document says:

> [We resolve] to call autochthonous American nations (including black nations) to join the common goal of God's mission for the world, so that, united, those of us living in dire situations and having common goals throughout the continent may seek, from evangelical perspectives and our own contexts, the dignity of all people and cultures of the world.[14]

This is the principal challenge to note from the experience narrated herein, which is articulated in resolution 8 of the Otavalo Declaration: that indigenous communities are subjects of the mission of God. They are no longer objects of mission, as they were for many years. Now, in these postcolonial times we are living, evangelical churches the world over must open up to the work of the Spirit and recognize that the Spirit breathes with new breath over minority peoples

14. Federación Ecuatoriana de Indígenas Evangélicos, "Declaración de Otavalo," in Fraternidad Teológica Latinoamericana, *CLADE III: Tercer Congreso Latinoamericano de Evangelización, Quito 1992* (Mexico City: FTL, 1992), 865–66.

and cultures. Likewise, we must recognize that the road of justice in the kingdom of God must take new routes, include new actors, and traverse new scenery. Holistic mission as incarnated in the October 2019 indigenous protest in Ecuador adopted a face that was different from the traditional ways of doing mission. As pastor Jesiel Carvajal described it, "Social protest is the new face of holistic mission."[15] Holistic mission must be reworked in light of this series of protests, and its starting point should be the needs of minority groups, like the indigenous peoples of Ecuador, and the ways in which they are carrying out God's mission.

'Social protest is the new face of holistic mission.'

15. Jesiel Carvajal, comment in the FTL gathering, "Evangelical Churches in the Socioeconomic Reality of Ecuador," October 24, 2019.

Bolivia: A Glance at the Current Context

Eva Morales and
Drew Jennings-Grisham

The State of the Nation

Bolivia is a landlocked country in central South America of some 424,164 square miles that gained its

Eva Morales, a psychotherapist and psychologist, is a doctoral candidate in missiology. She lives in Bolivia, where she and her family work in defense of human rights and lead a house church in their neighborhood. For many years Eva was the general secretary of the Bolivian chapter of IFES. A long-term member of the FTL, she has served as president since 2016.

Drew Jennings-Grisham, a nationalized Bolivian from the United States, served alongside several indigenous churches in Bolivia for seven years. He and his family recently moved to Medellín, Colombia, where they serve with Paz y Esperanza and Memoria Indígena. Drew has been a member of the FTL for several years.

75

independence from Spain in 1825. With a population of 11.5 million inhabitants,[1] the country's history has been marked by political instability, territorial wars with neighboring countries, military rule, and the struggle to establish democracy since the 1980s. On February 7, 2009, as part of the national transitions unfolding under the government of Juan Evo Morales Ayma, the country was declared to be plurinational and was officially renamed the "Plurinational State of Bolivia."

Bolivia's constitutional capital is the city of Sucre, where the judicial branch of the government is head-quartered. The executive and legislative branches and the administrative functions are headquartered in the city of La Paz. Both seats of government are in the western, Andean regions of the country. The department of Santa Cruz, located in the eastern side of the country, is the region where agroindustry is strongest, and it is there where the country's economic power is concentrated. This distribution of powers that corresponds with geographic and ethnic regions has generated political, economic, and ethnic (*colla* vs. *camba*[2]) tensions and confrontations as different worldviews and visions for the country collide. Thus, the country is in many ways split into two opposing factions: La Paz/western/*colla* vs. Santa Cruz/eastern/*camba*.

---

1. See the homepage of the Instituto Nacional de Estadística de Bolivia (INE) for population estimates, updated daily: https://www.ine.gob.bo/index.php.
2. *Colla* refers to those living in the western part of the country, most often identified with people of indigenous background; *camba* refers to those living in the eastern part and is most often identified with lighter-skinned descendants of Europeans, the *criollos*.

To better understand the country's internal tensions, it is necessary to know that, in changing the country's name to the Plurinational State of Bolivia, Bolivia is trying to make visible and recognize the dignity of the various people groups who inhabit Bolivian territory as well as recognize their right to cultural identity and self-determination.[3] In addition to the mestizo mix of European descendants, Bolivia's peoples include thirty-six indigenous[4] groups and thirty-six linguistic groups besides Spanish spread across the four geographic regions: the Andean altiplano, the sub-Andean valleys, the eastern plains, and the Amazonian region of the north.[5] Though precise figures are difficult to establish due to differences in census terminology and methodology, it is estimated that Bolivia's population is between 40 and 60 percent indigenous.[6]

It is estimated that Bolivia's population is between 40 and 60 percent indigenous.

3. Juan Carlos Durán Böhme, "Del estado multicultural al estado plurinacional," *Revista Boliviana de Derecho* 8 (July 2009), 31, http://www.redalyc.org/pdf/4275/427539907003.pdf.
4. In this essay, "indigenous" refers to those who self-identify with a particular ethnic population descending from the original peoples that populated the American continents at the time of the European conquest, as well as those who, without necessarily considering themselves indigenous, come from a community or cultural group whose customs, beliefs, and practices reflect the cultures of such original people groups.
5. Ministerio de educación, "Lenguas indígenas originarias: Idiomas oficiales del Estado Plurinacional de Bolivia," (La Paz: 2014), 4, 7, https://www.educabolivia.bo/files/textos/TX_Lenguas_Pluri.pdf.
6. Sybila Tabra, "Bolivia: Resultados del Censo 2012 causa polémica por reducción de población indígena," *Servindi*, August 8, 2013, https://www.servindi.org/actualidad/91607.

77

Political Context

Evo Morales was the country's first indigenous president, and he came to power with majority support in parliament and received nearly 54% of the vote,[7] a level of confidence rarely seen in Bolivian history. The resounding support he received came primarily from the rural indigenous classes who achieved this feat in conjunction with the middle class and intellectuals. The more equitable distribution of social capital achieved by the Morales government is undeniable and has caught the eye of the world. Advances in improved health care, education, access to basic services, and legal equality and inclusion for minorities have led to Morales being "seen as a Nelson Mandela of South America."[8] However, the political legacy of Morales is rife with controversy, and last November he fled the country in the midst of explosive conflict.

After nearly fourteen years in power, Evo Morales attempted to run for an unconstitutional fourth term in the October 20, 2019 elections, trusting in his overwhelming popularity in rural areas to secure another term in office. Public confidence in election transparency and fairness was already very low before the elections because of Morales's candidacy that was in blatant opposition to the constitution and his broken promise to respect the national referendum of

---

7. International Foundation for Electoral Systems, Election Guide, "Bolivia: Election for President: Dec. 18, 2005," http://www.electionguide.org/results.php?ID=183.

8. Ernesto Londoño, "'This Will Be Forever': How the Ambitions of Evo Morales Contributed to His Fall," *The New York Times*, November 11, 2019, https://www.nytimes.com/2019/11/11/world/americas/evo-morales-bolivia-resignation-coup.html.

February 21, 2016, in which the populace voted against allowing Morales to bypass constitutional term limits. Another factor for public mistrust of the elections was the fact that the entire Electoral Supreme Court had been handpicked by the MAS-dominated government (MAS: Movimiento al Socialismo, Movement toward Socialism, the party of Evo Morales), and it was this court that eventually approved Morales's candidacy.

These factors proved toxic when voting irregularities were pointed out on election day. Accusations of fraud and protests began immediately, and controversy raged regarding the need for new elections. After losing the support of the police and military, Morales, his vice president, and the presidents of both houses of Congress resigned and fled the country. Because all three people in the constitutional line of succession had resigned, Jeanine Áñez—from the tropical lowlands of Bolivia, second vice president of the Senate, and member of the opposition party, Democrat Social Movement—became president of a transitional government tasked with holding new elections.

Deep social wounds and divisions between ethnic groups, social classes, and political agendas remained.

The entire conflict rapidly demonstrated that deep social wounds and divisions between ethnic groups, social classes, and political agendas had not been healed by the advances in inclusion of indigenous and peasant groups and the developments made by the MAS government. The new government did not help try to bring unity or healing to the situation. Instead, it quickly moved to dismantle many of the former

79

MAS-controlled government's policies both domestic and foreign and proclaimed it would "bring the Bible back into the government"—a claim that suggests they want to take indigeneity out of the government.[9]

New elections are set to be held in May 2020, but the country is more fragmented than ever. Old wounds are reopening, reflected not only in the number of candidates but also in the struggle for power within the MAS party. After the longest-ever presidency in Bolivian history, there is much uncertainty and speculation about the future. Questions abound regarding whether the advances of the MAS-controlled government will hold or just how many scandals will be uncovered, and whether right-wing political and economic interests will take advantage of the situation.

Economic Context

Bolivia is a socialist state open to the free market. Sidestepping all the debate that these postures generate, Bolivia has achieved a remarkable reduction in rates of extreme poverty: from 38.2% in 2005 to 15.2% in 2018.[10]

Bolivia has no access to marine ports, which are so critical for exports and imports. Even so, its 4.3% economic growth for 2019 was projected to place it as the

---

9. Philip Reeves, "Bolivia Struggling to Transition to New Elections Following Fall of Evo Morales," NPR, November 25, 2019, https://www.npr.org/2019/11/25/782732943/bolivia-struggling-to-transition-to-new-elections-following-fall-of-evo-morales.

10. INE, "Bolivia entre los países de la región que más redujo la pobreza", March 12, 2019, https://www.ine.gob.bo/index.php/component/k2/item/3383-bolivia-entre-los-paises-de-la-region-que-mas-redujo-la-pobreza.

third highest-growing economy in Latin America, just behind the Dominican Republic (5.5%) and Panama (5.4%).[11]

Bolivia is currently considered a middle-income country given that moderate poverty was reduced from 60.6% in 2005 to 36.4% in 2018[12] and extreme poverty was more than cut in half, as noted above. These are the lowest levels registered in the country's history.[13]

Bolivia achieved a remarkable reduction in rates of extreme poverty between 2005 and 2018.

In the midst of this macroeconomic growth, the middle class and private business sectors express discontent over the perceived corruption of the Morales government. Despite the country's achievements, this dissatisfaction led to Carlos Mesa (former vice president under Gonzalo Sánchez de Lozada, who led the government when Sánchez was forced to resign until Mesa, too, was forced to resign due to violent protests) rising as the second strongest political force in the country in the 2019 general elections. Mesa was one of many other opponents considered to be representatives of the traditional political right.

11. AméricaEconomía.com, "Rep. Dominicana, Panamá y Bolivia liderarán el crecimiento económico en A. Latina en 2019, según la Cepal," April 11, 2019, https://www.americaeconomia.com/economia-mercados/finanzas/rep-dominicana-panama-y-bolivia-lideraran-el-crecimiento-economico-en.

12. Xinhua, "Pobreza extrema en Bolivia disminuye 23% en 13 años y alcanza su nivel más bajo," *AméricaEconomía.com*, March 12, 2019, https://www.americaeconomia.com/economia-mercados/finanzas/pobreza-extrema-en-bolivia-disminuye-23-en-13-anos-y-alcanza-su-nivel-mas.

13. Ibid.

81

Social Context: Drug Trafficking and Corruption

Bolivia is immersed in a never-ending struggle against drug trafficking, ranging from control over the production of coca to the control, pursuit, and sanctioning of drug traffickers themselves. A 2010 report from the Bolivian representative of the United Nations Office on Drugs and Crime (UNODC) confirmed there were 19,000 hectares of illegal coca being cultivated in the country; according to the peasant farmers, they have no idea where their harvest ends up.[14] Since then, the Morales government passed a 2017 coca law that increased the authorized, legalized area of coca cultivation to 22,000 hectares.[15] Under the framework of this conception of legalized growing, the latest UNODC report states that there were 23,100 hectares being cultivated in 2018.[16] Regardless of how the data is evaluated, Bolivia is a narcotics-producing country. The area of Chapare in the tropical region of Cochabamba is the heart of coca production in the country. Any casual observer can note the booming economic activity of the region. Recent reports indicate that high-purity cocaine is brought in by small airplanes from Peru and, together with the coca from

Bolivia is a narcotics-producing country.

14. UNODC, "ONU: Bolivia existe 19 mil hectárea de coca excedentaria" (2010) https://www.unodc.org/bolivia/es/press/mundo_coca.html.
15. Cat Rainsford, "Bolivia Coca Growers Fight for Control of Legal Production," Insight Crime, August 13, 2019, https://www.insightcrime.org/news/analysis/bolivia-coca-growers-fight-for-control-of-legal-production/.
16. UNODC, "Latest UNODC Monitoring Report shows decline of coca cultivation in Bolivia," August 22, 2019, https://www.unodc.org/unodc/en/press/releases/2019/August/latest-unodc-monitoring-report-shows-decline-of-coca-cultivations-in-bolivia.html.

Chapare, is turned into coca paste or into pure cocaine by itinerant laboratories located in the region of Santa Cruz, to then be taken to Paraguay and Brazil, from where the cocaine is sent to Europe and the United States.[17]

In the first half of 2019, details came to light linking high-ranking political officials with drug traffickers.[18] One of the cases that shook the country involves the Cartel Jalisco Nueva Generación, considered one of the most dangerous cartels on the planet. One of the cartel's leaders, José González Valencia, was living freely and unencumbered in Bolivia despite the fact that the United States was offering $5 million for information leading to his capture. With false identification, González conducted business in the country's largest livestock markets, purchased properties, and entered and exited the country at his leisure until the Brazilian government arrested him.[19] González's comfortable stay in Bolivia would not have been possible without the blind eyes of countless officials.

---

17. Williams Farfán, "Tres de las 17 rutas de la droga pasan por Bolivia," *La Razón*, April 22, 2019, http://www.la-razon.com/nacional/seguridad_nacional/rutas-droga-pasan-Bolivia_0_3134086581.html (accessed January 10, 2020); Mariano Bartolomé and Vicente Ventura Barreiro, "El papel de Bolivia dentro de los esquemas del tráfico de cocaína," Real Instituto Elcano, August 11, 2019, http://www.realinstitutoelcano. org/wps/portal/rielcano_es/contenido?WCM_GLOBAL_CONTEXT=/elcano/elcano_es/zonas_es/ari102-2019-bartolome-ventura-papel-de-bolivia-dentro-de-esquemas-del-trafico-de-cocaina.
18. See, for example, Página Siete Digital, "Caso narcopolicías: Medina distinguió a otro implicado en narcotráfico," *Página Siete*, May 7, 2019, https://www.paginasiete. bo/seguridad/2019/5/7/caso-narcopolicias-medina-distinguio-otro-implicado-en-narcotrafico-217338.html.
19. Daniela Castro, Nelfi Fernández Reyes, and Guilherme Amado, "Las dos caras del capo de la droga de México que se escondió en Bolivia," *El Deber*, July 1, 2019, https:// eldeber.com.bo/143232_especial-las-dos-caras-del-capo-de-la-droga-de-mexico-que-se-escondio-en-bolivia.

83

Through high ranking police officials, officers of justice, judges, district attorneys, and government employees, the Bolivian state is implicated in corruption linked to drug trafficking. The corruption of public servants, including senators and members of parliament, is evident in cases in which government ministers have had to answer for actions of their subordinates. One such case is that of former interior minister Carlos Romero, who faced questioning while he was still in office in conjunction with the scandal of rigged admissions into police academies. Four former chiefs of police are facing trial for presumed involvement in the criminal network that rigged the admissions.[20]

The MAS party systematically divided grassroots organizations that criticized the government's policies.

The government of Evo Morales was also guilty of direct interference of the executive branch in the legislative and judicial branches, as well as the electoral supreme court, thus concentrating the power of the government and of the MAS political party.[21] To further concentrate MAS power, throughout Morales's presidency the MAS party systematically divided grassroots organizations that opposed or criticized the government's policies or projects. MAS created parallel institutions, such as the coca growers of Chapare, the Central

20. Ángel Guarachi, "Aplazan para el 29 de junio interpelación al ministro Romero por denuncias contra policías," *La Razón Digital*, May 21, 2019, http://www.la-razon.com/index.php?_url=/nacional/seguridad_nacional/policia-narcotrafico-carlos-romero-ministro-vinculos-corrupcion_0_3151484863.html.

21. Susana Seleme Antelo, "La corrupción en la Bolivia de Morales. Parte 1," Eju.tv, March 28, 2019, https://eju.tv/2019/03/la-corrupcion-en-la-bolivia-de-morales-parte-1/.

Obrera Boliviana (Bolivian Worker's Center), and the Bartolina Sisa National Federation of Peasant Women of Bolivia, that were willing to support the party line. These parallel organizations caused much confusion and mistrust about leadership in local communities and rendered powerless many indigenous, environmental, and workers' grassroots organizations. With the recent dramatic changes in Bolivia, it remains to be seen how these groups will be restructured, reorganized, restored, or splintered further.

The Morales government also created many state-owned industries in an attempt to stimulate the local economy and shift the economic focus from exporting raw materials to producing finished goods. However, access to government funds for these enterprises has often led to corruption and white elephant projects left abandoned. Yet the success of government efforts to reduce poverty and improve access to healthcare and education, especially in the rural Andean region, has led many to say they are willing to ignore some political leaders' faults, and so they continue to support MAS.

The State of the Church

Religion in Public Discourse

With the transformations the country has undergone under Evo Morales and the adoption of the new constitution in March 2009, Bolivia became a secular state,

85

thus severing the official hegemony of the Catholic Church over political processes. Article 4 of the new constitution guarantees religious freedom for all beliefs and religious dogmas practiced in the country.

The government of Evo Morales, through the adoption of the new constitution, catalyzed the reclaiming of identity among original people groups. This came about through official recognition of the practices of indigenous spiritualities and the worship of Pachamama (Mother Earth, the goddess of the land and of agricultural fertility). Political events became Aymara and Quechua religious spaces. Events like the Aymara New Year celebration, Aymara religious and political inauguration ceremonies celebrating each of Evo Morales's presidential terms, and others among these Andean communities were televised nationally with government support. However, there was a notable lack of support for and public presence of other indigenous spiritualities, such as those from the lowlands among the Ayoreo, Guaraní, and Chiquitano peoples. This disparity was due to internal political problems among indigenous groups. The result was a reduced presence of other religious expressions in government events like interfaith services as well as the imposition of Andean spiritual practices through public education.

Catholicism and Protestantism

In Bolivia, the Catholic religion arrived through the sword and the cross. Paria was the first Spanish settlement and is about seventeen miles northeast of the city of Oruro, in the middle of the altiplano plateau of the Andes. It was founded on January 23, 1535 by captain Juan de Saavedra, and, by decree of Diego de Almagro, the Catholic religion and baptism were imposed on all inhabitants.

Recorded history names Allen Gardiner as the first Protestant missionary to Bolivia, from 1845–1847. He arrived at what is now the Department of Tarija and Sucre. His attempts to establish relationships with the native population and his passionate preaching in the streets of cities inhabited by a Catholic population bore no fruit, and the first efforts of the evangelical church to establish a presence in Bolivia came to naught.[22]

The Protestant evangelical church in Bolivia as we know it today has its roots in other early Protestant missionaries who arrived to preach and distribute Bibles in the country. Protestant presence includes Mennonites, Lutherans, Adventists, Baptists, Pentecostals, Methodists, free churches, and others, and foreign missionaries remain active in Bolivia.

Over 90 percent of the population self-identifies as either Catholic or Protestant.

Surveys and research studies demonstrate that Bolivia's population is between 71 and 81 percent Catholic, between 16 and 21 percent Protestant, between 1 and 4 percent

22. Arnoldo Canclini, "En Bolivia: 1845–1848," in *Hasta lo último de la tierra: Allen Gardiner y las misiones en Patagonia* (Buenos Aires: La Aurora, 1951), https://archive.org/stream/hastaloultimodel00canc/hastaloultimodel00canc_djvu.txt.

unaffiliated, and between 2 and 3 percent "other."[23] It is clear that while Roman Catholicism remains the primary religious identification in Bolivia, Protestant evangelicalism is not insignificant. And all the data indicates that Bolivia primarily identifies with the Christian religion. In the Plurinational State of Bolivia where between 40 and 60 percent of the population is indigenous, over 90 percent of the population self-identifies as either Catholic or Protestant.

Both the Catholic and Protestant evangelical churches have public presence in education, health, and media sectors, including schools, colleges, universities; hospitals that provide specialized services in major cities; and radio, television, and other means of mass communication.

Certain Catholic-Protestant evangelical alliances have arisen in recent years, including the prolife movement PROVIDA. PROVIDA defends the traditional concept of the family against abortion and the expansion of rights for sexual minorities. The movement, which has arisen among Catholic and Protestant evangelical fundamentalist groups, has been used and manipulated by right-wing political sectors. For example, in the recent October 2019 general elections,

23. See Carla Paz Vargas, "Bolivia: Destacan el elevado índice de cristianos en el eje central; el 81% es católico," April 23, 2011, https://eju.tv/2011/04/bolivia-destacan-el-elevado-ndice-de-cristianos-en-el-eje-central-el-81-es-catlico/; Wilma Pérez, "Mayor porcentaje de católicos y cristianos lo conforman jóvenes," La Razón, April 20, 2014, http://www.la-razon.com/index.php?_url=/sociedad/Mayor-porcentaje-catolicos-cristianos-conforman_0_2036796350.html; Pew Research, "Religion in Latin America: Widespread Change in a Historically Catholic Region," November 13, 2014, https://www.pewforum.org/2014/11/13/religion-in-latin-america/.

a Korean-Bolivian evangelical pastor and doctor, Chi Hyung Chun, entered the race very late in the process and ran on an antiabortion, anti-LGBTQ, anti-indigenous religion platform. He ended up winning over 8 percent in the polls for a solid third place above other candidates who were more well-known and had campaigned much longer.[24] Chun, now a presidential candidate for the May 2020 elections since the October 2019 results were annulled, has declared that "Christians will now get their turn" after MAS's attempts "to return to communism."[25]

This resurgence of political-religious fundamentalisms in Bolivia begets alliances which become obstacles that stamp out the practice of incarnational, contextual mission and that push the church to assume ideological and political postures. The theological discourse and actions of the so-called "prolife and pro-family" movements are directed against abortion and homosexual marriage and in defense of the traditional interpretation of the family. Yet they do not address the real issues of inequality and suffering that are experienced by those who fall outside the paradigm of the traditional family.

We must recognize that versions of a prosperity gospel have flooded our region with leadership that is hierarchical and manipulative in mainly Pentecostal

24. Fernando Molina, "El factor Chi Hyun Chung en el escenario electoral boliviano," *El País*, October 21, 2019, https://elpais.com/internacional/2019/10/21/america/1571629165_240801.html.
25. ABI, "Chi Hyun Chung suma su candidatura a las elecciones presidenciales con el FPV," *Los Tiempos*, January 29, 2020, https://www.lostiempos.com/actualidad/pais/20200129/chi-hyun-chung-suma-su-candidatura-elecciones-presidenciales-fpv.

89

and neo-Pentecostal churches. So-called prophets and apostles abuse their authority and manipulate people's consciences with theologies that promote emotional and spiritual codependence as well as a commodification of the faith for the material benefit of the leaders. Even in churches that are not in the Pentecostal vein, Protestant leadership models tend to be hierarchical and patriarchal, which has set the stage for Protestant and evangelical believers to easily fall prey to manipulation and authoritarianism.

Protestant and evangelical believers easily fall prey to manipulation and authoritarianism.

Indigenous Spiritualities

As has been mentioned, another important religious reality in Bolivia are the religions of the original people groups, primarily the Aymara and Quechua. While some would consider these in the "other" category in the religious surveys cited above, a great number of those who practice indigenous spiritualities also practice Christianity.[26] In academic settings, some indigenist extremists call for the eradication of any and every form of the colonizers' religion in the attempt to reclaim their ancestral beliefs; yet many indigenous Bolivians combine aspects of their ancestral religions with Catholic or Protestant Christianity. In general, the religions of original people groups see

26. See Marcelo Vargas, "Bolivian Aymara Neo-Pentecostal Identity: Historical Background and Case Study Analysis of the Power of God Church," *Journal of Latin American Theology* 9, no. 1 (2014): 9–71.

the spiritual and physical worlds as one integrated whole, and spiritual beings or forces are active in all aspects of life and all places. Inherent in their world-view is the protection of cities by the *apus*, which are the protective divine mountains that stand guard over a city or region.

Yatiris and *amautas* are common in cities in the western part of the country. These are a sort of priest/healer/wise man combination who are guides for the ceremonies held for Pachamama or other spirits depending on what is needed: healing and personal or familial prosperity, etc. While traditionally a *yatiri* would never ask for payment, through the indigenous concept of reciprocity he would always be compensated in some way over time. However, the services of *yatiris* have become commercialized and monetized in cities today.

Another common belief is in Ekeko, the Aymara god of abundance. His feast day on January 24, traditionally celebrated in the markets of Alasitas, has become popular throughout the country. Similarly, celebrating the Aymaran New Year on June 21 (*Willka Kuti*, the return of the sun), which marks the start of a new solar cycle at the arrival of the winter solstice, is now common. A 2009 supreme decree declared the day an official government holiday, and the festival has been

Many indigenous Bolivians combine aspects of their ancestral religions with Catholic or Protestant Christianity.

91

held in the ruins of Tiwanaku with the support of the Morales government every year since.[27]

Throughout the history of Catholic missions and presence in Bolivia, as well as the spread of Protestantism, multifaceted syncretism has arisen. This is seen poignantly in the association of the indigenous concept of Pachamama with the Virgin Mary. In carnival season every February, special offerings are made to her.

Faithful Obedience to God in Public Spaces

Corruption abounds on all sides in Bolivia, and all too often the church seeks to protect a narrow conception of its own interest instead of safeguarding the interests of God's entire creation. Examples of people who manage to practice kingdom values in the public sphere while staying clean from corruption are rare.

In 2009, Bolivia was restructured as a plurinational state and officially became a secular state. Ten years later, after arduous work among interreligious commissions, the freedom of religion law was passed on April 10, 2019.[28] The Asociación Nacional de Evangélicos de Bolivia (ANDEB, National Association of Bolivian Protestants), in which around 80 percent of Protestant

---

27. For discussion on the issues surrounding this holiday, see Javier Aliaga, "Año nuevo aymara 5.527: ¿Cómo nace y por qué genera polémica en Bolivia?", *France24. com*, June 20, 2019, https://www.france24.com/es/20190620-ano-nuevo-aymara-polemica-bolivia.

28. "Ley de Libertad Religiosa: Conoce los artículos más destacados de la norma," *El Deber*, March 29, 2019, https://www.eldeber.com.bo/bolivia/Ley-de-Libertad-Religiosa-conoce-los-articulos-mas-destacados-de-la-norma-20190329-0011.html.

denominations in Bolivia participate, was active in this process.

During nearly a decade of work among the interreligious commissions, ANDEB maintained its representatives and continued to prioritize active participation in the interreligious groups working to pass the freedom of religion law. As part of the process, the Protestant representatives had to concretely engage in dialogue and deal with religious tolerance in the face of the variety and diversity of expressions of indigenous spiritualities. This would have been a wonderful opportunity for Bolivia's rather conservative evangelical churches to undergo a parallel process of biblical theological reflection regarding engaging other religions and spiritualities in the public square. Unfortunately, this process did not occur. Though it was based more on a desire to protect the interests of conservative evangelicals than on a call to engage the public square with a holistic Christian vision, ANDEB's participation in the crafting of the law is admirable.[29] Other Protestant sectors rejected the law entirely, interpreting it as state control over their churches and a return to the previous century when the state was entwined with religion.[30]

ANDEB's participation in crafting of the freedom of religion law is admirable.

29. Prensa de la Cámara de Diputados, "La Asociación Nacional de Evangélicos de Bolivia aseguró sentirse incluida en la Ley de Libertad Religiosa," Cámara de Diputados, March 12, 2019, http://www.diputados.bo/prensa/noticias/la-asociaci%C3%B3n-nacional-de-evang%C3%A9licos-de-bolivia-asegur%C3%B3-sentirse-incluida-en-la-ley.
30. Ángel Guarachi, "Bloque de evangélicos rechaza proyecto de Ley de Organizaciones Religiosas," *La Razón*, March 12, 2019, http://www.la-razon.com/sociedad/iglesias-evangelicos-rechazo-ley-organizaciones-religiosas-proyecto_0_3109489065.html.

93

A truly inspiring case of Christian witness was the former Methodist bishop Rolando Villena who, from 2010 to 2016, served as the ombudsman of the Plurinational State of Bolivia. In preparation for becoming a candidate, Villena resigned from his position in the Methodist Church. After being invited by Evo Morales and approved in Congress, he took up the challenge of being the people's defender, or ombudsman. From the beginning of his service, Villena determined to be an impartial defender and to take up the cause of any citizen or institution whose rights had been violated. Both the population and the media recognized the value and integrity of how he carried out his duties. Throughout his tenure, he faced political pressure from the executive branch to skew his actions in favor of the state and to the detriment of those suffering harm, as was seen in the emblematic cases of the brutal repression of indigenous peoples in Chaparina in 2011 and the plans to build a highway through indigenous lands in the Isiboro Sécure Indigenous Territory and National Park (TIPNIS).[31]

The Catholic Church in Bolivia tends to speak up and insert itself in an unlimited number of ways and regarding any and every issue. In contrast, the Protestant evangelical church displays a marked lack of focus on social issues. Unless social issues are perceived as affecting traditional family values—as in the issues to which PROVIDA has served as a response—or are

31. Christian Rojas Villagomez, "Villena: Mi designación como Defensor fue política," May 6, 2016, *Urgentebo*, https://www.urgentebo.com/noticia/villena-mi-designaci%C3%B3n-como-defensor-fue-pol%C3%ADtica.

perceived as an existential threat to the church—as in the case of ANDEB's motivation to help craft the freedom of religion law—, evangelical leadership generally remains silent in Bolivian political life. Limiting their political involvement to instances of perceived threat means they rarely if ever speak up on behalf of other oppressed groups. Rolando Villena's admirable political involvement was the effort of a single person while the church as a whole remained silent on these issues. In the case of the conflict in the TIPNIS, for example, the media attention did not get evangelicals motivated to defend indigenous rights. Instead, churches began to send missionaries and do short-term evangelism trips! It was a short-sighted response with a reduced gospel.

> *Evangelical leadership rarely if ever speaks up on behalf of other oppressed groups.*

What the Church Needs to Hear and to Share

Voices to and from the Worldwide Church

In our current globalized, postmodern context, developing biblical theological reflection regarding Christian spirituality in dialogue with other spiritualities is crucial. The Andean region and, in particular, Quechua and Aymara theologies have made great contributions to this dialogue. The church's experiences in Bolivia can be instructive to churches going through similar processes in other parts of the world. Yet while it can be helpful to others, at the same time

95

the Bolivian church needs help in this regard as well, especially among our more conservative members. We need to hear testimonies, life experiences, and theological reflection related to the subjects of interculturality and indigenous spiritualities. There is great need for learning more about the dialogue between Christian spirituality and other spiritualities. The Bolivian church would likewise benefit from theological reflection and life experiences related to tolerance and religious dialogue in the context of a secular state, such as how churches in Europe or other regions have navigated or are navigating the surrounding cultural waters. Equally crucial is for the Bolivian church to hear experiences of Christian witness in the defense of human rights within totalitarian states.

Within Latin America, much work has been done within the Fraternidad Teológica Latinoamericana (FTL, Latin American Theological Fellowship) in the subjects of justice and gender equality, theologies of hope, theological reflections on male tenderness and masculinities, and biblical models for life. It is crucial for Latin American churches to wrestle toward a theology that frees men and women from patriarchal, *machista* frameworks expressed in the "Latino macho man" stereotype, which is undergirded by biblical interpretations in conjunction with cultural beliefs and practices. This damaging framework is manifested in the high levels of generalized violence throughout our continent. Latin America is in desperate need of a theology of tenderness and hope in contexts of violence, and the work of the FTL can help greatly here.

When the Rooster Insists on Crowing: Church, State, and Human Rights in Contemporary Brazil

Marcus V. A. B. de Matos

Introduction

This article is not intended as a full report on the current and complex situation of church and society in Brazil. Instead, I will mainly write about things I have

Marcus V. A. B. de Matos has a PhD in law and is the secretary for the National Board of Aliança Bíblica Universitária do Brasil (ABUB), the Brazilian student movement affiliated with IFES. He is the head of teaching programs at the Judicial School of the High Labor Courts in Rio de Janeiro.

97

experienced or observed in the past three years and briefly relate them to the history of the church in Brazil. The aim here is to give a narrative to historical and current facts that directly affect the Brazilian church, especially Protestant and evangelical[1] denominations and their affiliated organizations. To add academic weight to this personal narrative I will also include findings from a research project I conducted from 2005 to 2010 in the Institute for the Study of Religion (ISER), in Rio de Janeiro.[2] The project gave me the opportunity to interview seventeen evangelical pastors who had been arrested during the country's most recent military dictatorship (1964–1985). The project has been both an inspiration and a frustration, as we only had enough funding to finish editing the video of one of the filmed interviews.[3]

My method is what one can call "participatory obser-vation," in which the observer is located inside the observed group or community.[4] Or, as we might say in this case, following Giorgio Agamben, when the observer is "caught" by an *apparatus*: a network of power relations

---

1. In this article, "Protestant" and "evangelical" are used as overlapping categories. In Brazil the official data on religious minorities usually merges Protestant and evangelical denominations. The conceptual division considered relevant for the purposes of this paper is between "mainline/traditional" and "neo-Pentecostal" evangelicals.
2. The initial findings of this project were published in 2014. See Priscila Vieira Souza and Marcus Vinicius Matos, "'Colorir o passado com o presente': Proposta de construção e apropriação de memória no Projeto Juventude, Política e Religião: Diálogos Intergeracionais," *Sociedade e Cultura* 16, no. 1 (February 6, 2014), https://doi.org/10.5216/sec.v16i1.28219.
3. Marcus V. A. B. de Matos, *Cristo e o processo revolucionário brasileiro* (Institu-to de Estudos da Religião [ISER], 2007), DVD, https://www.youtube.com/watch?v=xxxshAqA7C8.
4. José Vargas, *Sociologia* (Porto, Portugal: Porto Editora, 2002), 119–20.

determined by government bodies, NGOs, realpolitik, the media, and ecclesiastical institutions.[5] This method, which is generally applied by anthropologists in ethnographic studies, "requires that researchers simultaneously observe and participate (as much as possible) in the social action they are attempting to document."[6] At the same time, I concede the methodological challenge of attempting to maintain enough intellectual distance from my object of study, the relationship between church and state in contemporary Brazil, and describing events in which I took part.

I left Brazil in 2012 for a PhD in the United Kingdom. I had been granted a full scholarship by the Brazilian Ministry of Education, a type of scholarship that had been available since the 1970s but has now been suspended by the recent budget cuts in education. It was the heyday of the Brazilian economy, when the employment rate was almost 100 percent. The Brazilian GDP was greater than that of countries like France and the UK. By June 2013, however, the scenario had shifted dramatically. Long lasting international economic crises had (once again) made the commodities price drop, and in Brazil this precipitated a huge political crisis. First, massive demonstrations took place, led by youth and social movements on the left and right.[7] Later, this took the form of a deep probe into

5. See Giorgio Agamben, *"What Is an Apparatus?" And Other Essays* (Stanford, CA: Stanford UP, 2009).

6. Lynne Hume and Jane Mulcock, *Anthropologists in the Field: Cases in Participant Observation* (New York: Columbia UP, 2004), xi.

7. See Marcus Giraldes, *O acaso e o desencontro: das manifestações de 2013 ao golpe de 2016* (Rio de Janeiro: Garamond, 2017), 28–39.

99

corruption, involving board members of the oil giant Petrobras; then it turned into a rigorous investigation of engineering and construction companies and their ways of donating money to politicians from across the political spectrum. Finally, the crisis came crashing down on the ruling party: PT, the socialist-labor party, was about to see its most important leaders go to jail.

Led by a public prosecutor who was also a Baptist leader, Deltan Dallagnol, a vast number of churches supported this activity. At first, those probing the corruption claimed that people from all parties were being investigated and prosecuted, and that it was just a movement against corruption in politics—something that churches should support. However, within a few years, it became clear that there was another kind of corruption going on in the investigations themselves. Judges were biased against left-winged parties. Prosecutors were engaged in a complex process of forging evidence to arrest certain politicians and then turning a blind eye to similar issues when they affected right-winged politicians they supported.[8] The judiciary proved biased,[9] and prosecution was crucial to determining the results of the 2018 presidential elections in favor of an extreme right candidate: Jair Bolsonaro. As a last move to complete the

There was another kind of corruption going on in the corruption investigations themselves.

8. Ernesto Londoño and Letícia Casado, "Leaked Messages Raise Fairness Questions in Brazil Corruption Inquiry," *The New York Times*, June 10, 2019, https://www.nytimes.com/2019/06/10/world/americas/brazil-car-wash-lava-jato.html.

9. Travis Waldron, "Brazil's Anti-Corruption Superstar Faces a Scandal of his Own," *HuffPost Brasil*, June 1, 2019, https://www.huffpostbrasil.com/entry/sergio-moro-lula-brazil-operation-car-wash_n_5d14f870e4b082e55365fe72.

scenario, the judge Sérgio Moro, who had become a hero for the anticorruption movement, accepted the invitation from the president he helped get elected to become attorney general, head of the Brazilian Department of Justice in the new administration.

As a result of the support gained through the popularity of the former judge, it seems that most of the Brazilian church, including the Catholic sector, has been co-opted by the current administration. How did we get to this point? I will argue that the alignment of the Brazilian church with the powers that be is not only the result of a poor choice to conform to the world it was supposed to change but is also a deliberate choice to promote the right-winged, colonial, and racist politics that have historically compromised its witness. And this choice has been made in at least three specific moments in our history. The rooster has crowed three times to warn us, Brazilian evangelicals and Protestants, of our denials of Jesus, as in Luke 22:61–62: "Then Peter remembered the word the Lord had spoken to him: 'Before the rooster crows today, you will disown me three times.' And he went outside and wept bitterly." How bitterly have we wept? What have we learned? This essay attempts to answer these questions by briefly examining the role of Protestant and evangelical churches in Brazilian society.

The alignment of the Brazilian church with the powers that be is a deliberate choice to promote certain politics.

101

When the Rooster Crowed the First Time: Amerindians and Africans, Slavery and Social Segregation

We have to start with colonialism. This critique falls harder on Roman Catholics, who were there from the beginning. The area that came to be known as Brazil was colonized by the Portuguese, and slavery was understood as the only way to maintain the colonizers' power over the vast land they took and its production. First, colonizers began to enslave (and rape) the natives. The cross and the sword went hand in hand. Together, Christianity and colonialism would shape the face of the "new" land. Rape was used as a powerful weapon, as it was believed that the mixed-race children that would emerge would want to be on the stronger side of the colonization war project. Jesuit priests who opposed rape were expelled from the country.[10] However, after the Portuguese conquest of parts of Africa, there was a shift in this strategy.

Slavery was understood as the only way to maintain the colonizers' power over the land and its production.

African slavery proved more profitable than that of the native Brazilians, despite being more expensive. The natives knew their own land: where to walk, what to eat, how to survive and fight back. Africans taken from another continent did not possess these

---

10. Marcos Roberto de Faria, "Contradições de uma missão: A legislação e a expulsão dos jesuítas de São Paulo em 1640," *Revista Histórica do Arquivo Público do Estado de São Paulo* 30 (April 2008), http://www.historica.arquivoestado.sp.gov.br/materias/anteriores/edicao30/materia01/.

skills when brought to a foreign land. So, while Jesuit priests were claiming that native Brazilians had a soul and therefore could not be enslaved, the colonizers engaged in two strategies: the total extermination of native Brazilians and the slave trading of Africans. Since the colonizers were no longer allowed to enslave the natives, they attempted to wipe them out, and the strategy included a massive biological war, spreading European diseases among tribes. For labor, they turned to African slaves. Since they were considered property, slaves were usually spared from death by outright killing; yet working conditions were so extreme that, for a couple of centuries, Brazil was a place where more Africans died than were born.[11] And still the slave trade was profitable.

After independence from Portugal in 1822, abolitionist ideas began to spread among the new Brazilian elite, which included mulatto people—yet, as people of color gained prestige and influence, their portraits and images in newspapers and other public outlets were progressively lightened to intentionally misrepresent their actual skin tones. Resistance was strong among native and African Brazilian descendants, who developed capoeira, a martial art that was secretly practiced as a dance, to hide its power from the eyesight of the masters. African Brazilians and natives also had to mix their religion with Catholicism to protect themselves from their masters' persecution, and

11. Márcia Amantino, "As condições físicas e de saúde dos escravos fugitivos anunciados no *Jornal Do Commercio* (RJ) em 1850," *História, Ciências, Saúde-Manguinhos* 14, no. 2 (2007): 1377–99.

they ended up giving images of saints the names of their own deities.[12]

Protestants established themselves in Brazil in the late nineteenth century. Missionaries first suffered a great deal of persecution from their Catholic brothers and sisters. Then, after freedom of religion was granted, they sought to modernize the country. How can people engage in reading the Bible if they don't know how to read? Brazilian churches developed Sunday school programs in which they focused first on teaching people how to read.[13] They invested seriously in education. But there was the issue of slavery. To our shame, many Protestants engaged in slavery and the slave trade.[14] In the last decade of the nineteenth century, a sensible Portuguese/Brazilian princess of the new generation, Isabel, granted abolition to all slaves, a move that played a decisive role in the end of the Brazilian monarchy.

In the late nineteenth century, Protestants invested seriously in education.

Brazil was the last country in the world to abolish slavery. After formal abolition in 1888, a complex system of social segregation was devised, and a duality, based on an idea of the complementarity of races, was

---

12. Rafael de Bivar Marquese, "A dinâmica da escravidão no Brasil: Resistência, tráfico negreiro e alforrias, séculos XVII a XIX," *Novos Estudos CEBRAP* 74 (2006): 107–123.
13. Antônio Gouvêa Mendonça, *O celeste porvir: A inserção do protestantismo no Brasil*, 3rd ed. (São Paulo: EDUSP, 2008), 99–101.
14. Elizete da Silva, "Visões protestantes sobre a escravidão," *Revista de Estudos Da Religião* 1 (2003): 1–26.

theoretically affirmed.[15] In this context, Protestants dropped their modernizing and progressive agenda too quickly and adapted themselves to the reigning (and overwhelming) social inequality that would shape the country for the next century and beyond.[16] I believe that the role of the church in giving in to racism and slavery during these first three hundred years, from 1600 to 1900, marks the first time the rooster crowed in Brazil. What would the church learn from this experience? At first glance, to depart from racism. But how long would that last? Would faith in the Word be stronger than the church's commitments to institutional powers? We have to look at a later chapter in history to find out.

The role of the church in giving in to racism and slavery for three hundred years marks the first time the rooster crowed.

When the Rooster Crowed a Second Time: The Church and its Support for the Dictatorship

After the monarchy, the Brazilian Republic emerged in the beginning of the twentieth century polarized between the new elites in power. On one side, liberals

15. See Gilberto Freyre, *The Masters and the Slaves: A Study in the Development of Brazilian Civilization* (Berkeley, CA: University of California Press, 1986). For a critique of these views, see Mauricio Lissovsky and Marcus V. A. B. de Matos, "The Laws of Image-Nation: Brazilian Racial Tropes and the Shadows of the Slave Quarters," *Law and Critique* 29, no. 2 (2018): 173–200, https://doi.org/10.1007/s10978-018-9222-2.
16. Antonio Gouvêa Mendonça, "O protestantismo no Brasil e suas encruzilhadas," *Revista USP* 67 (2005): 48, https://doi.org/10.11606/issn.2316-9036.v0i67p48-67.

believed that the state should not intervene in land and private property. Once in power, they decided to burn all documents concerning slavery to avoid revenge (and damage claims) from its victims.[17] On the other side, Positivists, and, later, Fascists, Nazi sympathizers, and Integralists[18] succeeded them in power, while socialist and communist parties were declared to be illegal. But democracy eked along, survived World War II, and was more stable after 1945. Freedom of religion was a fact, and ecclesiastical debates turned to the (never tired, it seems) dichotomy between social justice and gospel proclamation.

However, the 1960s would kill democracy. In 1964, supported by the USA and fearing the influence of Cuba and the Soviet Union in Brazil, a military coup took place. Fueled by Cold-War fear of communism, Catholics, Protestants, and evangelicals joined a broad alliance with liberals, conservatives, and Fascists to resist the socialist and labor government. With their support, the Brazilian army took down the government of the democratically elected Workers' Party president, João Goulart.[19] Churches removed ministers and youth leaders who were considered leftists from institutional positions of power. This broad alliance, widely supported by the CIA, planned to take the (supposed) communists out of power and then hold new elections.

---

17. Evandro Piza Duarte, Menelick de Carvalho Neto, and Guilherme Scotti, "Ruy Barbosa e a queima dos arquivos: as lutas pela memória da escravidão e os discursos dos juristas", *Universitas JUS* 26, no. 2 (2015): 24, doi: 10.5102/unijus.v26i2.3553.
18. Integralists were those who followed a Brazilian version of Fascism.
19. Elio Gaspari, *A ditadura envergonhada*: *As ilusões armadas* (São Paulo, Brazil: Companhia das Letras, 2002), 44–77.

In the process, many churches turned members accused of leftism or communism over to the army, and countless were subsequently tortured.[20]

The regime soon fell into the hands of the Fascists, the "hard line" of the Brazilian army, comprised of Nazis, Integralists, and former supporters of Mussolini. In 1968, an emergency act suppressed all civil liberties. It is important to note that there was a legislative structure in place all this time, overseen by a controlled parliament and confirmed by a biased judiciary that was supposed to give legitimacy to this fake democratic regime. But killing democracy has a price that is also paid by the dominant classes.

As the political struggles intensified, middle-class white students, along with Catholic priests and nuns, began to be illegally detained, tortured, raped, and made to "disappear." Church members and clergy on the Protestant side who then decided to go against those now leading the regime suffered the same fate. In all this, part of the liberal elite turned against the government. Similarly, Catholics withdrew support from the regime. But evangelicals and Protestants by and large maintained their support. In doing so, they ostracized their youth leaders either to the ecumenical movement or to the Communist party. These young Christians would find a human rights agenda outside the church to fight the regime.

Evangelicals and Protestants by and large maintained their support for the dictatorship.

---

20. Rodrigo Cardoso, "Os evangélicos e a ditadura militar," *IstoÉ*, last updated January 21, 2016, https://istoe.com.br/141566_OS+EVANGELICOS+E+A+DITADURA+MILITAR/.

107

Eventually, young people took up arms. Several guerrilla and terrorist groups were established, some supported by the Soviet Union, others by Cuba or China, and one with links to Algerian freedom fighters. In a short span of five years, most of these groups were utterly defeated. On top of that, 434 people were executed or disappeared;[21] 1000 bags of human remains from that time are still to be identified;[22] and an estimated 8,350 native Brazilians were killed in the Amazon forest while the army attacked guerrilla fighters.[23] Also significant, around 20,000 people were tortured.[24] The general then in charge of intelligence affairs had an ethical explanation for his policies: "We torture, so we don't have to kill that many people."[25] As the violence mounted, the Catholic Church, along with a few Protestant organizations, assumed a frontal opposition to the regime.[26]

By 1976, the ground had shifted again. In the USA, Jimmy Carter, a born-again Christian, was elected president. He believed that a strong defense of human rights around the world would help bring down the USSR. But this strategy had political consequences for

---

21. Comissão Nacional da Verdade (CNV), "Comissão Nacional da Verdade: Relatório," vol. 3 (December 10, 2014), 26.
22. Daniel Wilkinson, "No Justice for Horrors of Brazil's Military Dictatorship 50 Years On," Human Rights Watch, December 13, 2018, https://www.hrw.org/news/2018/12/13/no-justice-horrors-brazils-military-dictatorship-50-years.
23. CNV, "Relatório," vol. 2, 205.
24. CNV, "Relatório," vol. 1, 350.
25. Elio Gaspari, A ditadura encurralada (São Paulo: Companhia das Letras, 2004), 136.
26. Catholic Church, Torture in Brazil: A Shocking Report on the Pervasive Use of Torture by Brazilian Military Governments, 1964–1979, Secretly Prepared by the Archdiocese of São Paulo (Austin, TX: University of Texas Press, 1986).

the dictatorships the USA was supporting at the time. The very country that had financially and tactically supported the Brazilian army to develop technology for torture, illegal wiretapping, and the disappearance of bodies was now abandoning them to their own devices. The Carter agenda for human rights led to the resistance to dictatorships in Latin America.[27]

In Brazil, there was a huge mobilization against the military in power. The dawn of a new generation and a new kind of political struggle appeared. Just like in African and other Latin American liberation struggles, students, some churches, and trade unions were at the forefront of the political struggle. This was a time of student and worker strikes and of bishops facing arrest. The Amnesty Act of 1979 pardoned political crimes on both sides—the guerrillas and the army— and marked the beginning of the new democratic process that was, paradoxically, led by the last general to be president, João Figueiredo, who sent a clear message: "I am opening it [the regime]. I will beat and arrest whoever is against this move."[28] This paradoxical sentence was a message aimed not only at the now agonizing guerrilla freedom fighters but also at the right-wing and Fascist officers of the armed forces who were opposing the return of democracy. But, as a foundational new beginning, it opens up a few other

The Amnesty Act of 1979 pardoned political crimes on both sides.

27. Gaspari, *A ditadura encurralada*, 367.
28. Frima Santos, "Último presidente da ditadura, João Figueiredo foi a ponte para a democracia," last updated October 15, 2018, https://acervo.oglobo.globo. com/em-destaque/ultimo-presidente-da-ditadura-joao-figueiredo-foi-ponte-para-democracia-22249279.

109

questions. Can there ever be democracy like this? Can democracy really arise as a concession, an agreement, and a compromise? What would the evangelical and Protestant churches learn from this tragic experience of supporting a dictatorship? The so-called Brazilian "New Democracy" would provide answers to some of these questions.

When the Rooster Crowed the Third Time: The Rise and Fall of the Brazilian New Democracy

A new constitution was enacted by 1988. The Brazilian army went back to its barracks, and state police forces that had collaborated with the dictatorship were now expected to guarantee the rule of law. I was born during the end of the dictatorship. My generation has seen thirty years of democratic rule. But we are now worried by the coming to power of those who fought against democracy and were, at that time, defeated. Is democracy going to last? We do not yet have the answers. But we do know how we got here, and we will now examine this more recent historical information.

In the last thirty years, the church has settled into a political space in Brazil. While Protestant and mainline evangelical denominations retreated to their enduring institutions—such as Instituto Mackenzie in São Paulo and Escola Superior de Teologia in Rio Grande do Sul—, the political protagonists of the 1990s were Pentecostal and neo-Pentecostal churches. By the beginning of the twenty-first century, evangelicals accounted for nearly 20 percent of the population.[29] Representing the biggest religious minority in Brazil, these massive churches based their theology mainly on a prosperity gospel and managed to build huge empires which included television companies and political parties. For two decades, they have become the main political leaders in what is called the Frente Parlamentar Evangélica (the Evangelical Parliamentary Front).[30] Affiliated with several different political parties, evangelical representatives in the Front have supported and opposed different administrations, without any clear ideological criteria. Many have been accused of corruption, of mixing church and state affairs, and even of persecuting other minorities.[31] This somewhat troubling political arrangement lasted with relative stability until 2013.

The political protagonists of the 1990s were Pentecostal and neo-Pentecostal churches.

Massive youth demonstrations in 2013 destabilized the political scenario. The major political parties of

---

29. See Pew Research, "Brazil's Changing Religious Landscape," July 18, 2013, https://www.pewforum.org/2013/07/18/brazils-changing-religious-landscape/; and Pew Research, "Religion in Latin America: Widespread Change in a Historically Catholic Region," November 13, 2014, https://www.pewforum.org/2014/11/13/religion-in-latin-america.

30. Paul Freston, "Evangelicals and the Secular State in Brazilian Politics: Current Controversies in Perspective," in *Brazilian Evangelicalism in the Twenty-First Century: An Inside and Outside Look*, ed. Eric Miller and Ronald J. Morgan (Cham, Switzerland: Palgrave Macmillan, 2019), 25–26.

31. Anthony Boadle, "Evangelical Christians Gain Political Clout in Catholic Brazil," *Reuters*, June 9, 2013, https://www.reuters.com/article/us-brazil-evangelicals-idUSBRE95805120130609.

111

the center-left and center-right were accused of serious corruption. Unrest spread from youth movements to institutions, from workers to elite families. However optimistic the scenario looked at the time, the fallout was discouraging. The new social and political actors that emerged victorious from these demonstrations were those ousted from the previous democratic agreement of 1988: extreme right movements and conservatives. They took the lead in the Dilma Rousseff impeachment process that many considered a coup.[32] The narrative of the "2016 coup" became clearer as the lineup for the 2018 presidential elections was produced.

The "Car Wash Task Force" (força-tarefa da Operação Lava Jato), a prosecution and federal police joint task force, was set to investigate corruption in the government, political parties, and companies, particularly the Brazilian oil giant Petrobras. Although fighting corruption in Brazil is necessary, the task force was, from the very beginning, accused of bias for colluding with right-winged political parties and interest groups. The task force led by Dallagnol fast turned into a coordinated movement which supported the removal of President Dilma Rousseff in 2016 and worked for the main goal of right-winged political parties: the arrest of former president Lula da Silva. Sentenced by judge Sérgio Moro, Lula was out of the presidential election process in 2018. This was crucial for its result: the election of Jair Bolsonaro as president of Brazil.

32. Giraldes, *O acaso e o desencontro*, 72.

This result was achieved with heavy support from evangelicals. Though evangelicals are not solely responsible for Bolsonaro's ascent to the presidency, they have embarked on a dangerous ideological enterprise. They have also provided the Bolsonaro government with people and resources. While the majority of the evangelical church (especially Pentecostal and neo-Pentecostals) has focused on electing "corporate"[33] representatives for the legislative support of the government in the National Congress, conservative and more educated groups have taken a different strategy. Instead of gathering political support from megachurches and noisy television evangelists, these conservative evangelical minorities are offering the current administration an intellectual base—something that, it could be argued, it was really lacking.

Conservative evangelical minorities are offering the Bolsonaro administration an intellectual base.

These groups, organized around alternative and social media, are providing the government with personnel that emerge from new institutions focused on "intellectual," upper-middle-class, educated evangelicals. These groups are mainly formed by conservative Calvinists, and include, but are not limited to, the Association of Evangelical Jurists (ANAJURE); the Kuyper Foundation; L'Abri Brazil;[34] and the Brazilian Association for Christians in Science (ABC2). These

---

33. Freston, "Evangelicals and the Secular State," 26.
34. Gustavo de Alencar, "Evangélicos e a nova direita no Brasil: Os discursos conservadores do 'neocalvinismo' e as interlocuções com a política," *Teoria e Cultura* 13, no. 2 (2018), https://doi.org/10.34019/2318-101X.2018.v13.12428.

113

institutions are all examples of groups that have organized support for and provided personnel to the Bolsonaro government. Their current associates (directors, presidents, vice-presidents, and so on) are now secretaries of state, officials, or advisors in the executive branch of power.[35] As a result of this open and almost unconditional support, they finally achieved something in the political agenda that was unthinkable a few decades ago: the idea of an evangelical justice in the Brazilian Supreme Court. Jair Bolsonaro has announced that one of his Supreme Court appointees will be "terribly evangelical."[36]

But, one could ask, what is so disturbing about evangelicals supporting the current administration's agenda in Brazil? Isn't it just the same as the evangelical support for Donald Trump in the United States? Isn't it similar to conservative Christians' support for prolife, profamily agendas worldwide? There are, of course, similarities between these new extreme-right politics that seem to be spreading worldwide, not only in their ideological agenda but also in their mobilization strategy. But there is a crucial difference in the ideological agenda that Trump promotes in the US, for example, and what Bolsonaro does in Brazil. In Trump's defense

What is so disturbing about evangelicals supporting the current administration's agenda in Brazil?

---

35. Ronilso Pacheco, "Quem são os evangélicos calvinistas que avançam silenciosamente no governo Bolsonaro," The Intercept Brasil, February 4, 2020, https://theintercept.com/2020/02/04/evangelicos-calvinistas-bolsonaro/.

36. Andreia Verdélio, "Bolsonaro Vows to Appoint Evangelical for Top Court," Agência Brasil, July 10, 2019, http://agenciabrasil.ebc.com.br/en/politica/noticia/2019-07/bolsonaro-vows-appoint-evangelical-top-court.

(reluctant, I confess), almost every time he has been accused of promoting racism or getting support from extremists, he has declared he opposes it, even when his declared opposition was clearly a lie and he seemed to have caused the problem from the beginning.[37] That is clearly not the case in Brazil.

The Brazilian president has openly declared his support for the most recent military dictatorship. In his impeachment speech against Dilma Rousseff (a woman known to have been brutally tortured during the dictatorship by the army), Bolsonaro publicly stated his praise for the only torturer from that time who was ever sentenced in a court in Brazil.[38] He promotes an extreme right-wing agenda that is compatible with free markets in economics but is authoritarian in politics. His agenda is extremely aggressive against human rights, and not only against the rights of women and minorities such as native Brazilians, African Brazilians, and LGBTQ communities; he is opposed to basic human rights like the rule of law and the right not to be tortured.[39] He is enthusiastic for brutality among police and security forces, institutions that have never really become democratic in Brazil and have been accused of torture, execution,

---

37. Frida Ghitis, "When We'll Know if Trump Means What He Says about White Supremacy," CNN, August 5, 2019, https://www.cnn.com/2019/08/05/opinions/when-well-know-if-trump-means-what-he-says-about-white-supremacy-ghitis/index.html.
38. G1, "Bolsonaro diz no Conselho de Ética que coronel Ustra é 'herói brasileiro,'" Grupo Globo, November 8, 2016, http://g1.globo.com/politica/noticia/2016/11/bolsonaro-diz-no-conselho-de-etica-que-coronel-ustra-e-heroi-brasileiro.html.
39. Frances Jenner, "Why Bolsonaro's Comments Matter," *Latin America Reports* (blog), August 14, 2019, https://latinamericareports.com/what-bolsonaro-says-matters/2906/.

115

and the forced disappearance of prisoners.[40] On top of that, the Brazilian president has been repeatedly accused of having family members (his sons) involved in corruption scandals that range from money laundering to association with and support from (and for) paramilitary forces in local governments, such as those who killed former city council member Marielle Franco.[41]

There seems to be an insurmountable number of reasons why the church and its institutions should depart from their acritical and enthusiastic support for the current administration. However, a brief look at the history of the church, and particularly of evangelicals in Brazil, shows that, to break away from those agendas, it would need more than just reason and common sense. It would, most probably, need to find new (or very old) theologies and certainly different leaders. Most significantly, it would need a renewed faith and to repent from its historical mistakes and sins. The rooster has crowed a third time, but, unlike Peter, the Brazilian church has not been listening. But a few Christians have. And we shall turn to them now.

The rooster has crowed a third time, but, unlike Peter, the Brazilian church has not been listening.

40. Dom Phillips, "Brazil: Tortured Dissidents Appalled by Bolsonaro's Praise for Dictatorship," *The Guardian*, March 30, 2019, https://www.theguardian.com/world/2019/mar/30/brazil-bolsonaro-regime-military-dictatorship.
41. Tom Phillips, "Bolsonaro in Spotlight after Photo with Marielle Franco Murder Suspect Surfaces," *The Guardian*, March 13, 2019, https://www.theguardian.com/world/2019/mar/13/jair-bolsonaro-paramilitaries-marielle-franco-suspects.

Resisting A Conclusion, or
Concluding for Resistance

Fortunately, the church is divided. The last sentence is, at minimum, a paradoxical one, in fact a very unlikely one. While it could be based on an optimist's approach to Paul's perspective on divisions (1Co 11:19), it is also a recognition that we have seen preachers and prophets denouncing the current situation. The co-optation and cooperation between church and state have not gone unnoticed and uncriticized. Nevertheless, those who resist and denounce are also those who are under heavier attack. Since before the election of Bolsonaro, lists have been made by private associations naming evangelical and protestant leaders considered "leftists," "communists," or aligned with the Workers Party (PT) and former administrations. Many of the people named in those lists have lost their jobs, and some have been unable to secure employment elsewhere.

Fortunately, the church is divided.

On the theological front, holistic mission (integral mission) has been under repeated attack in the last ten years, particularly the past five. Evangelical NGOs and missionary initiatives associated with integral mission, along with several church-based social services projects, have suffered more from these rhetorical attacks on their theological foundations—and on their financial support from the church. Naturally, in the present situation, it is expected that they would lead the way

117

in criticizing the current evangelical support for this government and its anti-human rights policies and record. However, these groups have never been fully supported by the political left (though that is one of the main accusations against them) and have no hold on major denominational institutions or leading churches. Hence, their resistance, instead of organized or coordinated, has most often sprung up on a case-by-case basis.

This was the case when a recent debate on racism, organized by the Baptist Youth Association (JBB), was cancelled against the will of the youth leaders. Atitude Baptist Church, in the west zone of Rio de Janeiro, is the church of Michelle Bolsonaro, the first lady. According to the media, church officials argued that the debate was "one-sided," probably referring to the left-right division in the church. The youth leaders argued: "If the debate is about racism, it can only have one side."[42] It was also the case when the federal police alleged that they found no traces of the murderers of the native Brazilian chief Emyra Wajãpi, in the Wajãpi reserve in the Amazon forest. This shocking lack of evidence set off an important player against the government: the Methodist Church, which quickly led the way in condemning the current government's police for actions against native Brazilians.[43] Needless to say,

---

42. Anna Virginia Balloussier, "Debate sobre racismo em igreja frequentada por Michelle Bolsonaro é cancelado," Folha de S.Paulo, July 19, 2019, https://www1.folha.uol.com.br/poder/2019/07/debate-sobre-racismo-em-igreja-frequentada-por-michelle-bolsonaro-e-cancelado.shtml.

43. Colégio Episcopal da Igreja Metodista, "Manifesto sobre a morte de indígenas brasileiros/as e outras violências," Igreja Metodista - Sede Nacional, August 2, 2019, http://www.metodista.org.br/manifesto-sobre-a-morte-de-indigenas-brasileiros-as-e-outras-violencias.

this is also the case with the shameless devastation of the Amazon forest that the current administration pretends not to see. In fact, it works hard not to see it, as in the firing of Ricardo Magnus Osório Galvão, the director of Brazil's space institute, for reporting what the satellites were showing: huge deforestation in the Amazon forest.[44]

Finally, I ask, when will the Brazilian church learn from its own history? How many times must the rooster crow before church leaders will repent and depart from their concessions to and support of political power? We do not know the answers to these questions, but we do know something from church and state history in Brazil: democracy always comes back. No matter how hard church and state work against human rights, God will not stand it forever. I would like to conclude by recalling Chico Buarque's song against the most recent military dictatorship, "Apesar de você," where the songwriter reminds us that authoritarian governments will never last. No matter how heavy repression is, it cannot stop water from springing, nor the rooster from crowing.[45] No matter how long it takes, the current arrangements and policies cannot and will not last. No matter how hard the government takes on the opposition; no matter how many Christians

How many times must the rooster crow before church leaders will repent and depart from their concessions to and support of political power?

44. Ernesto Londoño, "Bolsonaro Fires Head of Agency Tracking Amazon Deforestation in Brazil," *The New York Times*, August 2, 2019, https://www.nytimes.com/2019/08/02/world/americas/bolsonaro-amazon-deforestation-galvao.html.
45. Chico Buarque, "Apesar de você," side B, track 6 on the LP *Chico Buarque*, Polygram/Philips, 1978.

119

will be excluded from their churches or delivered up to torture and arrest—like the rooster who will always crow, the Holy Spirit cannot be restrained. The Spirit will blow wherever God wishes to (Jn 3:8), and those in power should know it. The rooster will insist on crowing, until repentance comes.

Paraguay:
A Young Population with a Hopeful Road Ahead

Flavio Florentín

The State of the Nation

In 1994, Pablo Deiros and Carlos Mraida published a short book titled *Latinoamérica en llamas* (Latin America in Flames), in which they discuss the movement of the Holy Spirit in the continent of Latin America. As I write this article, we are again in a moment when our beloved Latin America is in flames,

Flavio Florentín is a pastor and a theology professor at the Universidad Evangélica del Paraguay in Asunción. He completed theological studies in the Baptist Seminary of Buenos Aires and received his doctorate in history from the Universidad Nacional de Asunción. He has participated in CLADE III and IV and several regional conferences of the FTL.

121

but not necessarily as a result of the movement of the Holy Spirit; rather, it is due to interminable, high-impact social and political conflicts in nearly all our countries. Chile has been in social upheaval for months. Bolivia's president has resigned and fled the country as a result of political upheaval surrounding contested elections. Peru, Ecuador, and Argentina are constantly teetering on the brink of political and economic instability. In Brazil, a popular former president is free again after months of incarceration. Paraguay is no exception: in July, the country was on the verge of impeaching the president elected less than a year prior.[1]

Paraguay is located in central South America in a territory of some 157,000 square miles with a population of around 7.1 million. Half of the inhabitants are twenty-six years old or younger, which makes for a relatively young populace, and the population density is low at 44.9 people per square mile. A bilingual nation, the official languages are Spanish and Guarani, which indicates a social reality that must never be overlooked. Social, cultural, and religious interactions among the rural population of the country are carried out by and large in Guarani.[2]

---

1. Daniela Desantis and Lisandra Paraguassu, "Paraguay Lawmakers Back Down on Impeachment Threat after Hydropower Deal Annulled," Reuters, August 1, 2019, https://www.reuters.com/article/us-brazil-paraguay-dam/paraguay-lawmakers-back-down-on-impeachment-threat-after-hydropower-deal-annulled-idUSKCN1UR580.
2. Data from James E. Painter, R. Andrew Nickson, and others, "Paraguay," *Encyclopaedia Britannica*, August 29, 2019, https://www.britannica.com/place/Paraguay.

Political Context

As is the case with most Latin American countries, Paraguay's path of development has been slow, difficult, and not without significant setbacks. Paraguay's government is based on the office of the president, elected by popular vote for five-year terms, and a congress made up of a forty-five-member senate and eighty deputies who represent the seventeen departments that comprise the geographical and political distribution of the country. Each department has a governor and a departmental board, and each city has a mayor who organizes and manages issues of common life within the urban centers.

Political life in Paraguay has been far from stable in recent years. From its birth as an independent nation, the country has gone through five constitutions. On average, a constitution has lasted in Paraguay for about thirty-five years. The most recent was ratified in 1992, three years after the end of the thirty-five-year dictatorship of Alfredo Stroessner. Since 1989, Paraguay has experienced relative democracy with elected presidents. The current president is Mario Abdo Benítez, son of the former private secretary to Stroessner. Abdo Benítez took the presidential oath in August of 2018, and less than a year later was nearly removed from office due to a scandal related to the agreement governing the Itaipu hydroelectric plant shared with Brazil. Public opinion in general is that Abdo Benítez is entirely incompetent

On average, a constitution has lasted in Paraguay for about thirty-five years.

123

as an administrator of public affairs.[3] If this political suspicion on the part of the populace continues to be confirmed, the country will likely have to deal once again with the social drama of ousting a president elected by popular vote. For a country like Paraguay, facing a steep uphill climb in regard to development, such political instability is disastrously unhelpful.

The justice department is the governmental sector hardest to stabilize. Yet investments, security, and just relationships between people in the country are all dependent on its proper functioning. This is a sore spot for the country, which languishes under an excruciatingly slow and unreliable justice system. One statistic will suffice by way of illustration: nearly 80 percent of the incarcerated individuals cram-packed into the severely limited space of the country's jails have not actually been condemned and sentenced.[4] The country has been reprimanded and put under sanctions by international organizations for prison overcrowding and for the poor administration of justice. Recently, though, there have been encouraging signs that indicate a more positive future in this realm. Many judges and prosecutors have been caught, investigated, and

Paraguay has been put under sanctions for prison overcrowding and the poor administration of justice.

3. Mariel Cristaldo, "Paraguayan President's Popularity Plummets amid Brazil-Linked Political Crisis," Reuters, August 14, 2019, https://www.reuters.com/article/us-paraguay-president/paraguayan-presidents-popularity-plummets-amid-brazil-linked-political-crisis-idUSKCN1V421O.

4. ABC Color, "Casi 80% de presos sin condena," ABC Color, February 18, 2018, https://www.abc.com.py/edicion-impresa/judiciales-y-policiales/casi-80-de-presos-sin-condena-1676273.html.

condemned for questionable dealings in their administration of justice. Furthermore, the slow renovation of
the nine-member Supreme Court is occurring little by
little as fit, decent people without ties to the politicians
of the day are gradually incorporated. These signs are
indeed encouraging.

The 1992 constitution assigns a reduced role to the
military, and the military has adjusted to the political
changes more quickly than perhaps any other realm of
government. Even so, it continues to be a heavy drag
on the country's economy. In a public address, Abdo
Benítez slipped in a remark about how the role of the
military needs to be reframed, given its current idle-
ness. The national police are moderately well-received
by the general populace, although in recent years,
given the economic powerhouse of the illegal drug
trade, it has been marked by corruption scandals in
which high-ranking officials are involved in actions
that favor and even protect drug trafficking groups.
The purging of its ranks is continual, which gives the
impression that the country has still not yet hit upon
the most efficient way to fight against the scourge of
corruption within the sectors that supposedly provide
security and guarantee justice for all people.

Economic and Social Context

Agriculture and livestock are the country's primary
activities, which means that the vast majority of the
land is concentrated among very few owners. Crop

125

production and raising livestock have led to indiscriminate deforestation, and the natural resources and soil quality are adversely affected, just as the survival of disadvantaged groups is increasingly precarious. While specialists point to a stable macroeconomy, the distribution of wealth reveals the long-suffering faces worn down by poverty, the displacement of people from rural areas to cities, and a denigrated indigenous population that wanders the country's capital city begging for daily bread.

Agriculture and livestock have led to indiscriminate deforestation and increasingly precarious conditions for disadvantaged groups.

The indigenous population of Paraguay represents 2 percent of the country's total population. In that 2 percent, there are five linguistic groups in nineteen communities with legal status distributed throughout the country's two regions. The reality of the indigenous population in the dry, western region is very different from that of communities in the subtropical eastern region. This is due primarily to the programs of sustainable development and peaceful communitarian living implemented by Christian Mennonite communities living with the indigenous communities of the Paraguayan Chaco.

Like most developing countries, Paraguay is experiencing little advancement and low investment in the areas of health and education, two crucial realms for achieving socioeconomic development. School dropout rates remain very high. While official statistics paint the situation in a better light, the reality on the

126

ground is that of every ten people who begin primary education, usually only four finish high school, and perhaps only one of these continues on to higher education. The illiteracy rate hovers around 6 percent of the population. Access to public health services is free, but the coverage and infrastructure for healthcare are in critical state. Many times, people with more complex health problems end up depending on family members or their community to cover the costs of their treatment. This is just one demonstration of the solidarity that characterizes the Paraguayan population.

The coverage and infrastructure for healthcare is in critical state.

The State of the Church

Expressions of Christianity

Roman Catholicism was established in the country with the arrival of the Spanish conquistadors. There is a rich history of the presence and impact of Jesuit missions in the country and throughout the basin of the Río de la Plata. A detail of no little import is that the most recent constitution recognizes Paraguay as a secular state with no official religion. Even so, the Catholic Church continues to have an enormous impact and influence in the country. Over 80% of the population self-identifies as Catholic,[5] though this figure

---

5. Pew Research, "Religion in Latin America: Widespread Change in a Historically Catholic Region," November 13, 2014, https://www.pewforum.org/2014/11/13/religion-in-latin-america.

by no means indicates that such a large percentage of Paraguayan residents are ardently, actively practicing the Catholic faith. Regardless, nearly 500 years of Catholic presence on the continent has profoundly impacted and pervasively influenced the culture, education, and spirituality of the region.

Article 82 in the current constitution recognizes the key role played by the Catholic Church in the country's cultural and historical development.[6] We will discuss just two examples. In the first, education, the Catholic Church has played a formative role in primary, secondary, and university education. Until around thirty years ago, there were only two universities in Paraguay, one of which was run by the Catholic Church. The second area of greatest impact has to do with the social forms and common life of the general populace, that is, with cultural manifestations. For centuries, holidays and social gatherings centered around festivities celebrating the patron saint of a town or city. These were often the only opportunity for a community to gather together. This social experience—still present today—forms collective conscience, identity, and passions that in some cases degenerate into dangerous fanaticisms that prohibit the free expressions of other Christian experiences.

Centuries of Catholic presence have profoundly influenced the culture, education, and spirituality of the region.

A curious fact not to be overlooked and which could be interpreted as indicative of many things, and which

128

6. Paraguay Constitution, art. 82.

was important for the Catholic Church's impact on the country's political life, is that, in 2008, a former Catholic bishop assumed the presidency of the republic. Fernando Armindo Lugo Méndez was a Catholic bishop until the year before he began his active political career. The Catholic Church changed his status to a member of the laity so that he would be unencumbered for political action and could assume the presidency if he won the elections. His presidency marked the end of nearly sixty continuous years of the same political party (Colorado) being in power. Without further analysis, these facts alone demonstrate the ever-present influence of the Catholic Church in Paraguayan life.

There have been some signs of openness in the relationship between the Catholic Church and other Christian faiths present in the country. One such was the agreement and collaboration between the Catholic Church and Protestant evangelical churches regarding laws that protect life from conception, the traditional view of the family, and freedom of conscience. All of these laws were included in the 1992 constitution and, for now, continue to regulate the lives of the citizenry in these regards.

The arrival of non-Catholic expressions of Christianity dates back to the end of the nineteenth century and beginning of the twentieth. European migration created the first incursion of Protestants into the country. This came about through immigration policy that allowed and encouraged the arrival of foreigners who would settle and cultivate the huge tracts of

129

unproductive land. It is important to note that these Protestants who arrived as immigrants retained and practiced their faith, but they did not spread it. They simply maintained the cultural and religious values of their forebears while they developed large areas of the country and turned them into economic hubs.

Protestants who arrived as economic immigrants retained and practiced their faith, but they did not spread it.

After the Congress on Christian Work in Latin America held in Panama in 1916, North American Protestants became aware of the need and took up the call to reach Latin Americans with a liberating gospel. This North American Protestant evangelical expression reached Paraguay in 1918, and the route of education was the primary means of evangelization. Protestant evangelicals built and established a school that still impacts and shapes the families of the most privileged sectors of the country today. This school, called Colegio Internacional, is run by the Disciples of Christ and in 2020 is celebrating 100 years in the country.

Currently, membership in Protestant churches in Paraguay hovers around 8 to 9 percent. It is difficult to arrive at accurate figures since there is no institution or organization in charge of monitoring or charting the social development and spread of Protestant churches.[7] The Protestant church's presence became more visible

7. The 2002 Paraguayan census, which is the most recent census year with reliable data, puts the Protestant population at 6 percent (see DGEEC, "Principales resultados del Censo 2002. Vivienda y Población," 62, https://www.dgeec.gov.py/Publicaciones/Biblioteca/censo2002_muestra10/vivienda_poblacion_censo_2002.pdf). The 2014 Pew Research study estimates 7 percent (see Pew Research, "Religion in Latin America"). Experience on the ground indicates a slightly higher number by 2020.

starting in the 1950s. Its efforts were centered on planting and growing churches, education, mass media, Bible translations into native languages, community development projects, and, recently, the political life of the country. It is noteworthy that there are over 120 Protestant-affiliated schools registered in Paraguay. For a country with such a low percentage of self-declared Protestants, this number of educational institutions is significant. We must add to that number teacher-training institutions, technical colleges, and, for the past twenty-five years, the Universidad Evangélica, which offers schools of education, psychology, nursing, theology, music, and economics.

Education was the primary means of evangelization by North American Protestants in Paraguay.

Evangelical megachurches in Paraguay are nothing like those seen in Colombia or throughout Central America. There is only one church with more than 10,000 members; the rest are smaller communities of faith that average fewer than 100 members. This situation has helped the Protestant evangelical church in Paraguay avoid notorious scandals that damage its public image and the reputation of its leaders. On the other hand, the slow, difficult growth of Protestantism in the country increases the obstacles to sharing the faith and planting new churches. The Protestant church in Paraguay seems to be at a standstill.

The Protestant church in Paraguay seems to be at a standstill.

To grow, it needs to hear voices from outside its context encouraging it to keep proclaiming a liberating gospel

131

of hope that responds to the real needs of people and brings lasting change and growth now in the present.

Examples of Faithful Obedience to God in Public Spaces

The evangelical church in Paraguay, as has been seen in other countries, had a leader who dove into the political arena and attempted to be a presidential candidate. In 2011, the Mennonite pastor Arnoldo Wiens Duerksen left his position in the church to be a potential candidate for the office of president. Within his party (the Colorado party, which was not in power at that time), he agreed to step away from the bid and instead pursue a seat in the senate. He is currently serving as the minister of public works. He is moderately well accepted among the populace and is generally considered to be trustworthy and not susceptible to corruption. For a country steeped in the corruption of public officials and deeply suspicious of all politicians, Duerksen's example is highly esteemed. Yet one lamentable fact is that Arnoldo has nearly completely cut ties with his former community of faith.

Another positive experience of a Christian committed to his faith and carrying out a public leadership role is the current Paraguayan general director of the Itaipu hydroelectric plant. The plant is a renewable energy venture shared equally with Brazil. In recent months it has been the center of a difficult crisis involving politicians from both countries. To resolve the differences and reestablish trust with the citizenry, the government turned once again to Ernst Bergen, an evangelical Christian committed to his faith and to public service. From 2005–2007, without partisan maneuvering and with the support of his church, Bergen served a successful tenure as the minister of finance. In the Itaipu crisis, he was called upon again to head up an institution that finances many of the country's development projects.

Conclusion

The Protestant evangelical church in Paraguay, though still fragile and emerging, makes a significant contribution to the spiritual, social, and economic well-being of the country. There are many stories of faithfulness and commitment that need to be brought to light and shared so that a new generation of evangelicals can be inspired and committed to keep proclaiming and living out their faith in Christ Jesus.

Argentina: Crisis, Uncertainty, and Fragmentation

Juan José Barreda Toscano and

Diana Medina González

The State of the Nation

To talk about Argentina in the year 2020 is to speak of a country drowning in an economic crisis second in the region only to that of Venezuela; to speak of a country facing political uncertainty after a new president has assumed office; and to speak of a fragmented society that has seen quality of life plummet in recent years.

Juan José Barreda Toscano, from Peru, has a PhD from ISEDET. He is the Executive Director of Bíblica Virtual (www.biblicavirtual.com) and has served as a member of the FTL board of directors.

Diana Medina González has a master's in economic development and international cooperation from the Benemérita Universidad Autónoma de Puebla, Mexico. She is working on her doctorate in social sciences through FLACSO in Argentina.

To understand the vicissitudes of current realities in Argentina, we must first understand the political context. And, in Argentina, everything is political.

Argentina[1] is a vast country in South America that stretches over some 1.07 million square miles. Its nearly 45 million inhabitants are spread throughout 23 provinces and a federal capital district, though over 90 percent is concentrated in urban areas, the largest being Buenos Aires, Córdoba, and Rosario. Argentina's varied terrain includes rainforest in the northeast, the Andes mountain range in the west, arctic plateau in the south, beach towns in the east, dry plains in the central north, and vast stretches of grasslands called the pampas in the middle. Since independence from Spain in 1816, Argentina has been populated by waves of immigrants from all over the world, primarily Europe, the Middle East, and Asia. In the past few decades, immigrants have poured in from Latin American countries as well, most notably from Venezuela in recent years. Successive governments have continued the colonialist stance of aggression toward or neglect of the country's indigenous population, reaffirming a history of racism, colorism, and classism that prioritizes social benefits for those of lighter skin tones with European heritage. While the republican Constitution of 1853 still governs the country, Argentina has weathered the wild

Since 1816, Argentina has been populated by waves of immigrants from all over the world.

---

1. Data from Robert C. Eidt, Tuio Halperin Dongyi, and Peter A. R. Calvert, "Argentina," *Encyclopaedia Britannica*, last updated March 9, 2020, https://www.britannica.com/place/Argentina.

back-and-forth between oppressive military dictatorships and civilian administrations, which themselves
have swung violently between populist movements
and neoliberal stances. Corruption has marked nearly
every administration.

In 2015, Mauricio Macri became president against
a backdrop of ideological polarization in reaction to
Kirchnerism/Peronism. Macri's political endeavors
were characterized by connections with the business
sector, financial markets, and political marketing.[2]

In his term, Macri reincorporated neoliberal economics as the development model in Argentina. This
decision led to the country's reinsertion into the globalized market, a gradual economic adjustment of
public funds, loans from international organizations,
and the reduction of worker take-home pay. Such
measures are more in line with the political-economic
projects of the 1990s than they are with the post-2008
global scenario. All of this was undertaken without
actually resolving the problems lingering from the previous administration, like inflation, unstable exchange
rates, and corruption.[3]

The economic crisis that went hand in hand with
Macri's policies has hit every social class, though naturally the impact has been greater on the middle and

---

2. Gabriel Vommaro and Mariana Gené, "Argentina: El año de Cambiemos," *Revista de
ciencia política (Santiago)* 37, no. 2 (2017): 231–54, https://dx.doi.org/10.4067/s0718-
090x2017000200231.
3. See Daniel García Delgado, Cristina Ruiz del Ferrier, and Beatriz de Anchorena, eds.,
Elites y captura del Estado: Control y regulación en el neoliberalismo tardío (Buenos
Aires: Flacso Argentina, 2018), http://politicaspublicas.flacso.org.ar/wp-content/
uploads/2018/10/Flacso-Elites-y-captura-del-Estado.pdf.

lower classes who have watched their quality of life get flushed down the drain. While the country does maintain protectionist policies for healthcare and education, the crisis has led to the closing of countless businesses, and access to housing and food is increasingly difficult.

The social response to this scenario was fragmented. The workers movement, traditionally at the head of the Argentine social struggle, took no initiative. Instead, different social movements took the stage with their own particular agendas. In recent years, these have included the feminist movement represented in the "Ni una menos" ("Not one less") campaign and the National Campaign for the Right to Legal, Safe, and Free Abortion; as well as the traditional movement of the Mothers and Grandmothers of the Plaza de Mayo.

By the end of 2019, under the promise of a change in the economic and social direction, the Kirchnerist/Peronist platform won the elections again. Now under Alberto Fernández, the new administration is facing a government deep in debt, a precarious society, and an international context that eyes it with mistrust.

The State of the Church

Under the Constitution of 1853, which remains in effect today with only slight modifications, the government of Argentina recognizes an official state church. While the state maintains the freedom of religion, it cedes certain privileges to one religion in particular: Roman Catholicism.[4] As of 2014, an estimated 71 percent of the population self-identified as Roman Catholic. Evangelicals ("evangelical" and "Protestant" are basically synonymous in Argentina) account for an estimated 15 percent of the population, while the remainder are unaffiliated or "other."[5] A 2019 report indicates that Catholicism has decreased to around 63 percent, evangelicals have held steady around 15 percent, and the nonreligious sector has grown to nearly 19 percent.[6] The evangelical sector is represented by a variety of mainline denominations (nearly 15 percent of Argentine Protestants) but the majority (nearly 85 percent) is comprised of Pentecostal and neo-Pentecostal congregations.[7] These non-Catholic expressions run the gamut of conservative postures linked institutionally and financially to their counterparts in the United States and Europe; to more progressive, autochthonous communities of followers of Jesus that seek ecumenical collaboration across ideological lines; to independent megachurches controlled by

> *The government of Argentina recognizes an official state church, the Roman Catholic Church.*

---

4. Maximiliano Campana, *Políticas antigénero en América Latina: Argentina* (Río de Janeiro: ABIA, 2020), 20, https://sxpolitics.org/GPAL/uploads/Ebook-argentina_20200203.pdf.

5. Pew Research, "Religion in Latin America: Widespread Change in a Historically Catholic Region," November 13, 2014, https://www.pewforum.org/2014/11/13/religion-in-latin-america.

6. F. Mallimaci, V. Giménez Béliveau, and others, "Sociedad y religión en movimiento. Segunda encuesta nacional sobre creencias y actitudes religiosas en la Argentina. Informe de investigación, n⁰ 25" (Buenos Aires: CEIL-CONICET, 2019), 7, http://www.ceil-conicet.gov.ar/wp-content/uploads/2019/11/ii25-2encuestacreencias.pdf.

7. Ibid., 10.

139

authoritarian leadership and nourished by exploitative prosperity gospels; and everything in between. Given the historic relationship between the Catholic Church and the state inherited from the colonial model, evangelical expressions of Christianity have not typically had far-reaching political influence, yet this has begun to change in recent years. And with Francis I as pope since 2013, the Catholic Church's relationship with the Argentine state has changed significantly.

With Francis I as pope, the Catholic Church's relationship with the Argentine state has changed significantly.

Politically, the pope has shown a preference for Kirchnerism/Peronism (a platform he was critical of when serving as archbishop of Buenos Aires) and has distanced himself from Macri's policies. The cooling of the relationship with the national government was formalized in 2018 when the Catholic Church in Argentina announced it would no longer be receiving state funds.[8] This move arose in the context of the public push for clearer separation of church and state in Argentina.

At the ecclesiastic level, the pope has supported and encouraged the movement of "slum priests," a sector of young priests who work in the poorest neighborhoods of the country and are associated philosophically and experientially with the Movement of Third World Priests from the 1960s and 1970s. This has created a kind of parallel structure within the Catholic Church,

8. Sergio Rubin, "En medio de la frialdad con el gobierno, la iglesia renuncia al aporte económico del estado," *El Clarín*, November 3, 2018, https://www.clarin.com/politica/medio-frialdad-gobierno-iglesia-renuncia-aporte-economico_0_A8ljWhg_n.html.

which in turn generates internal tensions over the loss of the episcopate's political and social power.[9]

As the Vatican grew more distant, the Macri government found a political and electoral ally in the evangelical movement. In the Province of Buenos Aires, the Macri administration even began delegating to the evangelical church certain welfare policies like the distribution of food and medicine, roles which it has historically only called upon the Catholic Church to fill.[10]

Though it is still too early to measure their growth and influence, it is undeniable that evangelical churches with conservative postures are playing an increasingly active role in the social sphere. This is particularly true of the some 12,000 congregations that make up the Asociación Cristiana de Iglesias Evangélicas de la República Argentina (ACIERA; Christian Association of Evangelical Churches of the Republic of Argentina).[11] While the phenomenon of evangelical churches playing key roles in politics has been more noteworthy in Brazil

Evangelical churches with conservative postures are playing an increasingly active role in the social sphere.

9. See Juliana Andrea Arias, "El Grupo de Curas en Opción Preferencial por los Pobres: Los herederos del Movimiento de Sacerdotes para el Tercer Mundo" (thesis, Universidad Nacional de la Plata, 2016), http://www.memoria.fahce.unlp.edu.ar/tesis/te.1242/te.1242.pdf.

10. Mariano Obarrio, "El gobierno recurre a las iglesias para el reparto de alimentos y la contención social," *La Nación*, October 1, 2018, https://www.lanacion.com.ar/politica/el-gobierno-recurre-iglesias-reparto-alimentos-contencion-nid2177228.

11. See Alianza Cristiana de Iglesias Evangélicas de la República Argentina, https://www.aciera.org/aciera-nosotros/historia-y-declaraciones/.

141

or Guatemala, it has been progressing since the 1970s in Argentina.[12]

In the most recent decade, ACIERA's leadership has been drawn primarily, though not exclusively, from Pentecostal and neo-Pentecostal sectors. It has somewhat successfully promoted—without the need for political alliances—a conservative ethical agenda centered on gender identity, family, and sexuality. ACIERA was influential in halting the 2018 bill that would have decriminalized abortion, and the association also managed to get a few preferred candidates on the ballot for representatives, senators, and mayors in the 2019 elections.[13]

The phenomenon of conservative evangelicalism increasingly captures the attention of the academy, politics, and the press, who analyze it with various and contradictory interpretations of its risks and opportunities. The coverage has brought to light the internal disputes within the Protestant religious sphere in light of the growth of fundamentalist currents.

For their part, most evangelical churches of a more progressive bent are represented in the Federación Argentina de Iglesias Evangélicas (FAIE, Argentine Federation of Evangelical Churches). These congregations have a long history of involvement in the public

12. Marcos Carbonelli, "Los evangélicos y la arena partidaria en la Argentina contemporánea," *Estudios Políticos* 37, (2016): 195–96, https://www.sciencedirect.com/science/article/pii/S0185161616000093.

13. Sergio Rubin, "Poco a poco, los evangélicos comienzan a ganar espacio en las listas," *Todo Noticias*, June 23, 2019, https://tn.com.ar/opinion/poco-poco-los-evangelicos-celestes-se-abren-espacio-en-las-listas_972850.

sphere. Among their members are pastors involved in the struggle for human rights, for improved education, and for the separation of church and state; they are likewise involved in ecumenical organizations and groups for interreligious dialogue that work for peace and healthy coexistence. While their voices were not well received within the Macri administration, there is hope that they will be taken into greater consideration as the Alberto Fernández government makes decisions about the problems facing the nation's people.

Congregations in the FAIE have a long history of involvement in the public sphere.

Examples of Evangelical Involvement in Public Spaces

Evangelical ideological currents related to the prosperity gospel have powerfully influenced the way leadership and participants in conservative evangelical churches interpret political realities. Despite their involvement in certain political matters, the agenda of these sectors remains distant from the most overwhelming problems of the majority of the population: malnutrition, lack of safety in the face of rising rates of theft and assault, unemployment and underemployment, the unequal distribution of wealth, and discrimination, among so many other things. Their interests lie among matters that turn a blind eye to or

143

even thwart the needs of the vast majority of the population.

In the broader society, processes are unfolding toward diversity in the definition of family, the recognition of gender identity rights of transgender individuals, and the prevention of gender-based violence. In this context, conservative evangelical churches, together with self-proclaimed "prolife" organizations, are attempting to curb the progress of rights in these realms and the implementation of public policies regarding sexuality and reproduction.

The interests of the prosperity gospel lie among matters that thwart the needs of the vast majority of the population.

One clear example is the reaction to already established laws about what is called "holistic sexual education," *educación sexual integral* (ESI). ESI went into effect in Argentina in 2006. In 2018, thousands of people—largely representing conservative evangelical churches as well as Catholic churches and their respective leadership—marched in a demonstration led by the movement "Con mis hijos no te metas" (Don't Mess with My Kids), to protest the inclusion of gender ideology in sex education in schools.[14] While the protests have ultimately had no direct effect on altering the laws, and educational institutions with religious affiliation are still allowed to modify ESI according to their own ideologies,[15] these

---

14. "'Con mis hijos no te metas' reunió a miles de manifestantes," *La Voz*, October 29, 2018, https://www.lavoz.com.ar/ciudadanos/con-mis-hijos-no-te-metas-reunio-miles-de-manifestantes.

15. Ana Carolina Parma, "Los colegios católicos mantienen la alerta contra cambios en la ESI," *La Voz*, November 22, 2019, https://www.lavoz.com.ar/ciudadanos/colegios-catolicos-mantienen-alerta-contra-cambios-en-esi.

currents have garnered national attention and highlight the disparity between agendas.

Spheres like ACIERA and the "Con mis hijos" movement demonstrate a marked lack of dialogue and little interest in providing straightforward information that would allow those they influence to have a clear, thorough understanding of the situations being faced. Within the Argentine Christian milieu there seem to be no spaces with mass appeal in which discipleship is practiced with freedom of conscience and the right to make decisions based on being well-informed; no spaces that encourage building bridges of respect within a diversity of thought by finding elements held in common. These spaces exist within certain evangelical schools, but their impact is minimal. Meanwhile, what abound are polarized positions, accusations, and inaccurate information.

Polarized positions, accusations, and inaccurate information abound within the Christian milieu.

Opportunities and Hopeful Practices

Expressions like "conservative evangelicals" and "conservative churches" and the like are so charged that they can hardly do justice to all the cases and the various individuals within each church. One positive result of spheres like ACIERA and "Con mis hijos" is that, in recent years, not only social issues but also the church's involvement in matters affecting the citizenry within the larger society are viable topics now.

145

An increasing number of evangelicals are availing themselves of the right to dialogue with appropriate, factual tools and information regarding social problems. Younger generations are especially active in this regard, as seen not only in their involvement in different political parties and social movements but also in the formation of small groups within their churches for the purpose of dialogue and public engagement.[16]

Along the same lines, something that the previously discussed actions of groups like ACIERA and "Con mis hijos" have led to is that faith postures linked to politics are a factor that causes congregations to redefine themselves, especially in terms of how any given church participates in the public sphere. This can seem negative when considering the diversity within a congregation, yet it also encourages people who entered the church "wounded" to seek spaces that are healthier for them. This is often seen in a migration toward more progressive movements with a mission incarnated in the realities of the common people.

A third result of the recent social experiences of churches and politics in Argentina is that they have allowed us to recognize that many people within churches of a conservative and even fundamentalist bent do not share the positions of their leaders. This is why we must be more precise when describing the church as a whole and not fall into generalizing perspectives that do not allow for the coexistence of

16. One such example is the "Espiritualidad y Birra" ("Spirituality and Beer") group. See the group's Facebook page, https://www.facebook.com/espiritualidad.birra/.

variety within churches, especially among young people. We must recognize a growing awareness among those involved in churches that evangelical leaders do not necessarily represent the opinion of large sectors of their own churches. The fear of speaking up goes a long way in silencing groups that find themselves in disagreement with their leadership. In situations and spaces where greater freedom of expression is practiced, people tend to express their doubts and their desire for respect and are eager for accurate, trustworthy information. These are people who desire to participate in the changes that would lead to a healthier and more just society. The reality of this discrepancy between many churchgoers and their leaders has led to the rise of several communities of faith founded as spaces for support and for engagement around specific social issues. Likewise, it has given rise to social networks and movements of pastors and churches who, beyond the realm of their denominational affiliations, join together to serve God within the larger society.

A fourth aspect which is just beginning to be seen is that our current social and political intersection is pushing some evangelical churches to make internal changes as a community of faith, and they are getting involved in the public life of Argentina again—as institutions and not just as individuals who happen to go to church. They are starting to seek out a place from which they can give a living shape to the message of hope for other Christians. This is seen on a large scale in outlets like marches for human rights and, on the local level, in joint actions in cooperation

147

with neighborhood associations that work on behalf of society's marginalized members. Joint projects include things like community food pantries, youth centers, services for women suffering from domestic abuse, and others.

Finally, one of the most noteworthy facts about the current junction of political and religious spheres in Argentina today is an increase of NGOs run by evangelicals who are seeking justice and abundant life. This can be seen in the case of organizations that defend children, in civil associations that aid women suffering gender-based violence,[17] and ministries geared toward immigrants, among others. One noteworthy characteristic is how these groups work in collaboration with non-religious or non-Christian organizations. This openness and cooperation is enriching churches and Christian organizations in multiple ways, for example in awareness of God's presence in all of his creation, in the humility required for being a church that wants to support life rather than save the world, in becoming a church that is a servant of God and of the people within it, and in becoming aware that God alone saves. By joining with other service organizations, Christian churches and organizations are confronted with their own limitations and faults; at the same time, they have

Humility is required for being a church that wants to support life rather than save the world.

---

17. For example, the Asociación "Pablo Besson" (Pablo Besson Association), which for over twenty years has served immigrants and people in situations of domestic violence. See their website, http://abriendoelcamino.blogspot.com/.

the opportunity to be humble before others, learn from them, and be supported and strengthened by them.

Given all this, the lack of dialogue among Argentina's evangelical churches is sapping the possibilities of their growing with each other's help. This situation is reflective of evangelicals throughout Latin America, the polarization being large in other countries as well. We are aware of no countries in which there have been rich dialogue and actions of deep-hearted cooperation between sectors in which they share tools, agreements, and actions for the purpose of carrying out the mission God has entrusted to them. There are some examples of shared work, the overcoming of differences through dialogue and healthy coexistence, as well as nurturing a contextual spirituality rooted in the real problems of real people. These include international movements like the Red del Camino network and organizations like the Fraternidad Teológica Latinoamericana (FTL, Latin American Theological Fellowship) and World Vision. A newer endeavor in the educational field is Bíblica Virtual. For the past ten years, this platform has brought together professors from diverse Christian traditions that comprise a community of theological teaching and learning based on dialogue, collaboration, and diversity. These experiences can serve to inspire the evangelicals of Argentina to the degree that we are open to being surprised, to being encouraged to change what must be changed, and to being humble enough to learn.

> *The lack of dialogue among evangelical churches is sapping the possibilities of their growing with each other's help.*

149

Our times are full of difficulties and questions. Argentina is going through a period of uncertainty, in which evangelical churches—and evangelicals themselves on a personal level—have a historic opportunity to be involved in helping our nation overcome the huge problems we face as a people. This is an enormous opportunity for bearing witness to our Lord Jesus who came to bring true life.

Teopoesía /
Theopoetry

Luis Cruz-Villalobos is a Chilean poet and editor, clinical psychologist, and psychology professor at the Universidad de Talca. A PhD candidate (VU Amsterdam) developing a practical theology of post-traumatic coping, he is also the author of several academic works and a wide number of poetry books. See www.amazon.com/author/luiscruzvillalobos.

151

Tankas[1] desde un país en llamas

1

Arde mi país
Como arde un horizonte al poniente
Justo antes que acabe
Un día completo y lleno de demoras
Un día extenso y vaciado de amor

2

Arde en la noche
Y también en la mañana y al medio día
Arde como nunca
Pues no podía contenerse más el magma
De esta tierra cuya reina es la inequidad

3

Arde mi país
Y es una indignación de antaño guardada
Que enciende
El corazón mismo de las cansadas masas
Una aguda indignación callada y honda

4

Arde en paz
Pero también con oscura violencia
Arde por justicia
Pero también por mezquina venganza
Por un odio alimentado sin descanso

1. La tanka es un tipo de poema tradicional japonés que consta de cinco versos de 5-7-5-7-7 sílabas, aproximadamente.

5

Arde mi país
Como pidiendo la más plena justicia
Ante los faraones
Arde trayendo las diez plagas de pronto
Como de improviso para quienes reinan

6

Arde esta tierra
Llena de cantores y guerreros y poetas
Arde pidiendo luz
Que alcance ahora realmente para todos
Y una alegría que no se quede a medio camino

7

Arde mi país
Y yo me pregunto aquí en silencio
Cuánto falta
Para que este arrebol encendido
Se torne noche y luego clara mañana.

A días del estallido social chileno.
Santiago de Chile, 21-10-19[2]

2. Luis Cruz-Villalobos, "Tankas desde un país en llamas," October 21, 2019. Printed with permission. See "Tankas desde un país en llamas. A propósito de Chile. Poemas de Luis Cruz-Villalobos," Crear en Salamanca (blog), October 22, 2019, http://www.crearensalamanca.com/tankas-desde-un-pais-en-llamas-a-proposito-de-chile-poemas-de-luis-cruz-villalobos/.

153

Tankas[1] from a Country in Flames

1

My country burns up
Like a horizon at sunset
Just at the end of
A full day full of delays
A long day empty of love

2

It burns through the night
and the morning and midday
Like never before
No more holding back the magma
In this land of inequity

3

My country burns up
With ancient indignation long locked
Down which now ignites
The very heart of the tired masses
Their deep, keen, silenced fury

4

It burns with a peace
And with a dark violence
It burns for justice
And for petty, mean revenge
And ceaselessly fed hatred

1. The tanka is a traditional Japanese poetic form that consists of five lines in roughly a 5-7-5-7-7 syllable pattern.

5

My country burns up
Clamoring for full justice
Before the pharaohs
Burning with all ten plagues at once
A complete shock to those who reign

6

This land burns up
Land of singers, warriors, poets
It burns begging light
That's truly enough for all
And joy that won't be cut short

7

My country burns up
And I in silence wonder
Just how much longer
Till this burning afterglow
Turns to night and then clear dawn

Written days before the social outbreak in Chile.
Santiago, Chile, October 21, 2019[2]

---

2. Luis Cruz-Villalobos, "Tankas from a Country in Flames," translated and printed
with permission.

Call for Book Reviews

The *Journal of Latin American Theology* publishes reviews of books addressing topics pertinent to life, theology, and any area related to the Latin American and Hispanic experience of following Jesus. Please send submissions and inquiries to Lindy Scott, lscott@whitworth.edu. Book reviews do not have to be written by members of the Fraternidad Teológica Latinoamericana (FTL, Latin American Theological Fellowship). We are especially interested in reviews of the following books:

- *Apocalipsis* (4 vols), by Juan Stam, Editorial Kairos
- *A Tale of Two Theologians: Treatment of Third World Theologies*, by Ambrose Mong, ISBN 9780227176580
- *Dios nos habla a través de sueños*, Ricardo Zandino, ISBN 9789871355525
- *Engaging the World: Christian Communities in Contemporary Global Societies,* by Afe Adogamne, Janice McLean and Anderson Jeremiah, ISBN 9781908355218
- *In the Company of the Poor: Conversations with Dr. Paul Farmer and Fr. Gustavo Gutiérrez,* by Paul Farmer, Gustavo Gutiérrez, Jennie Weiss Block and Michael Griffin, ISBN 9781626980501
- *Mentalidad antidepresiva,* by Myriam Fervenza Meghruni, ISBN 9789871355532

- *Mission at and from the Margins: Patterns, Protagonists and Perspectives,* by Peniel Jesudason, Rufus Rajkumar, Joseph Prabhakar Dayam and I. P. Asheervadham, ISBN 9781908355133

- *Nuestra Fe: A Sourcebook for Latin American Christianity,* by Ondina González and Justo González, ISBN 9781426774263

- *Our Only Hope: More than We can Ask or Imagine,* by Margaret B. Adam, ISBN 9780227174685

- *Pentecostal Mission & Global Christianity,* by Wonsuk Ma, Veli-Matti Kärkkäinen and J. Kwabena Asamoah-Gyadu, ISBN 9781908355430

- *Protestantismo y política en la vida y obra de Juan A. Mackay,* by Tomás Gutiérrez, ISBN 9789972701924

- *The Rebirth of Latin American Christianity,* by Todd Hartch, ISBN 9780199843138

- *Seeing New Facets of the Diamond, Christianity as a Universal Faith,* by editors Gillian Bediako, Benhardt Quarshie, and Kwabena Asamoah-Gyadu, ISBN 9781908355591

- *Stopping the Traffick: A Christian Response to Sexual Exploitation and Trafficking,* by Glenn Miles and Christa Foster-Crawford, ISBN 9781908355515

- *Theologies of Liberation in Palestine-Israel: Indigenous, Contextual, and Postcolonial Perspectives,* by Lisa Isherwood and Nur Masalha, ISBN 9780718893613

Comentario Bíblico Contemporáneo

- ✓ Autores de toda América Latina
- ✓ Más de 160 especialistas
- ✓ La Biblia comentada libro por libro
- ✓ Bosquejo de cada libro
- ✓ Artículos contextuales
- ✓ Preguntas de reflexión
- ✓ Bibliografías
- ✓ Guía temática

Order form for the
Journal of Latin American Theology:
Christian Reflections from the Latino South

Name: _____

_____

Address: _____

_____

Email: _____

_____

Checks should be made out to Editorial Kyrios and sent to Lindy Scott, 1515 Riverside Avenue, St. Charles, IL 60174.

Subscription for *Journal of Latin American Theology*

Individual	_____	$35.00
Institution (USA)	_____	$80.00
Institution (Int'l)	_____	$100.00

Subscription for *La Serie FTL* (Spanish)

Individual	_____	$35.00
Institution (USA)	_____	$80.00
Institution (Int'l)	_____	$100.00

Total $_____

Convocatoria por los 50 años de la FTL

Concurso de ensayos

REPENSANDO IDENTIDADES EVANGÉLICAS EN AMÉRICA LATINA:

Contextos, contrastes y desafíos

Fecha límite
para postular:
20 de mayo

Consulta las bases en:
www.ftl-al.com

FRATERNIDAD
TEOLÓGICA
LATINOAMERICANA

Grupos de lectura
VIRTUAL

¡Reflexionemos juntas y juntos!

Celebrar los 50 años de la FTL es un proceso que inicia desde ahora

FRATERNIDAD
TEOLÓGICA
LATINOAMERICANA

Ilustraciones de: inconicbestiary y pikisuperstar